HOCKEY FOR SCHOOLS

PELHAM BOOKS FOR SCHOOLS

NETBALL FOR SCHOOLS
Joyce Baggallay

SWIMMING FOR SCHOOLS
A. H. Owen

CHESS FOR SCHOOLS
A. F. Stammwitz

CRICKET FOR SCHOOLBOYS
Phil Sharpe

SOCCER FOR SCHOOLBOYS
Harold Shepherdson

ATHLETICS: FOR STUDENT AND COACH
Ian Ward and Denis Watts

SUCCESSFUL RUGBY
Donald Ireland

BASIC FLORISTRY
Rona Coleman

JUNIOR PEARS ENCYCLOPAEDIA
Edward Blishen

HOCKEY FOR SCHOOLS

Carol A. Bryant

PELHAM BOOKS

First published in Great Britain by
PELHAM BOOKS LTD
26 Bloomsbury Street
*London, W.C.*1
1969

7207 0231 3

Printed in Great Britain by
Western Printing Services Ltd, Bristol

ACKNOWLEDGEMENTS

I am deeply indebted to Miss Beryl Marsh (Kent, East and England) for undertaking the writing and photographs on Goalkeeping, and for her patience and skill in producing the diagrams.

I would also like to express my thanks and appreciation to a number of people for their help and encouragement in presenting this book. In particular; Miss A. Hobbs, President of the All-England Women's Hockey Association, for writing the Foreword, Miss J. Whitehead, Miss P. Pattison, Miss B. Chapman, Miss E. Hall for reading the proofs and correcting the text. Lady Bawden, 'A' Umpire, whom I consulted on points of Umpiring. The East Anglian Women's Umpiring Sub-Committee for permission to reproduce the East 'C' Umpire Test Paper, and Mrs. M. Wilkins for the drawings. Some of the photographs are taken from my own collection—for the others, I am indebted to Miss B. Marsh, Miss J. Whitehead, Mr. and Mrs. H. Darbon, *The Kent and Sussex Courier*.

Finally, my mother, who deciphered and converted my longhand to a typescript, and who now thinks that had she known as much about hockey as she does now, she too would have been an International Player.

FOREWORD
by Audrey Hobbs
President of the All-England
Women's Hockey Association

In this latest book on Women's Hockey, Carol Bryant has set out to cover every aspect of the game and I hope this comprehensive study will find its way into many school libraries.

For those readers who do not know Carol Bryant, her own hockey career from School, through College, County, Territory, to the final honour of playing for England, has been marked by her great love and enthusiasm for the game. She is a specialist Physical Education teacher and coaches hockey both in this country and in the U.S.A. In this book she hopes to pass on some of the knowledge and skills gained through her years of experience, so that girls and teachers in schools everywhere can benefit.

Hockey is more than a mere game, for when its skills have been mastered it gives opportunity for travel, for friendships and for international goodwill. Carol Bryant was a member of the English Touring Team which I took for an unforgettable tour of South Africa and the Rhodesias in 1961. May the future England players who are now still at school be helped by this book to enjoy just such a tour in the 1970's.

INTRODUCTION

Hockey for Schools has been written in order to help young players and partly in appreciation of the opportunity for visiting other countries afforded to me as a member of the England Hockey Team. The experience has been tremendously stimulating both on and off the Hockey field.

The foundations of success in Hockey are invariably laid in Schools. Because I believe that so much can be done not only in teaching skills but in building up the right attitude and inculcating enjoyment and enthusiasm, I agreed to take on the task of presenting to Schools a comprehensive handbook. Consideration has been given to the individual enthusiast, Games and House Captains whose responsibilities lie in training teams, and Teachers, particularly those new to the organisation and coaching of the game within School.

The material is divided into two sections, the first part concerns the Game, and the second part contains information for the Teacher. The Rules book should be used to supplement the chapter on Umpiring as I have not tried to cover every infringement but have chosen to draw the readers' attention to the interpretation of specific rules.

Many books have been written showing individual techniques. However, not many Coaches lay sufficient stress upon choosing the right movement at the right moment. References are made to these moments and many of the diagrams are designed to illustrate these points in game situations. For clarity, some diagrams include only the immediate players, and it is important to bear in mind that the diagrams do not indicate clearly the amount of space there is on the field. The photographs, apart from those on Goalkeeping, are chosen to show skills occurring in match play.

Although the skills of hockey can be coached to a high degree of proficiency, and the creation of a happy atmosphere will stimulate enthusiasm, the real effort to succeed lies within the individual player.

CONTENTS

ILLUSTRATIONS

LINE DRAWINGS

Part One

1 Technique

To move with the ball is the first impulse on being given a stick and ball, and it is very interesting and heartening to see that out of a group of beginners many will look at home with a stick by the end of the first session. In this, the correct length and the weight of the stick is of great importance, together with good footwork and the basic running technique.

In moving with the ball (dribbling) the players should appear comfortable and uninhibited. You will soon discover that in order to have the greatest control over the ball, the stick should be gripped with the hands apart—the right hand almost halfway down the handle, the left hand easily gripping around the top. See Fig. 1.

Fig. 1. The grip for dribbling

Note the grip of the left hand particularly.

If the bottom hand is too low, the player will appear crouched; if too high, she will be almost upright with a flappy uncontrolled stick.

In dribbling, try to have the ball under control to do what you wish in any split second: the closer the ball is to the stick the better. On an excellent surface it is possible to place the stick behind the ball, push and let the ball roll immediately in front of it. However,

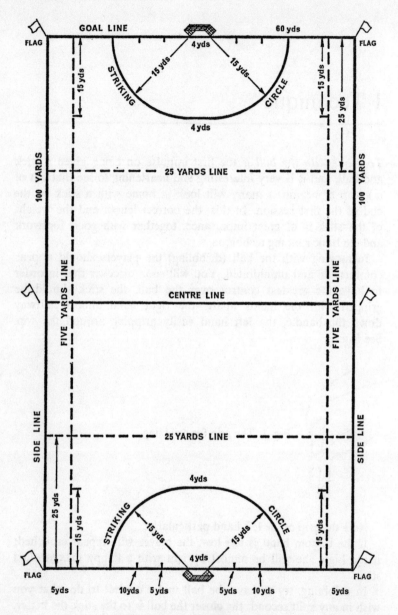

Fig. 2. Plan of a hockey pitch

on most grounds this is impossible as the ball is inclined to hop and pop, but the next best thing is the technique of short sharp taps with the ball as far away in front of the feet as can be managed.

Good positioning of the ball is vital—for only then will you

(1) be free to run with fast long strides and have no fear of kicking the ball,

(2) be able to see the opposition ahead in relation to yourself and the ball,

(3) have the ball in immediate possession to time your movements.

This ideal position can only be achieved by an easy but full extension of a strong left arm. It might be of interest to mention here that the left-hander does have an obvious advantage because her left arm is already the stronger; whereas for the majority, the left arm needs to be strengthened to cope with both the simplest and most advanced techniques. Once a player has had experience of the game, she will realise its importance, particularly the emergency techniques of lunging and jabbing, when the left arm does the work. There is also the obstruction rule to apply in emergency tackling: should the stick be held in the right hand, there is more likelihood of bodily contact.

Do not be content to run with the ball without considering its best position for the next move—for instance:

(1) if you are about to hit the ball to the right, be sure that over the final strides you are dribbling the ball on your right side,

(2) if you are about to hit the ball to the left, manoeuvre the ball across so that it is both in front of you and slightly to your left.

Practise swerving by

(1) moving the ball to either side, whilst running in a straight line,

(2) altering the relationship between the body and the ball by moving the feet either side of the ball.

PROPULSION

To propel the ball accurately is the next objective. A player should be able to make the ball move: fast, slow, with spin, and through the air, and, most important, be able to use these actions quickly, efficiently and at the right moment.

THE DRIVE (or HIT)

In order to make the ball travel fast and in the appropriate direction, the stick should punch the ball flat and firmly; in so doing the stick should become an extension of the arms and become pendulum-like in its action, but with the emphasis on the forward swing. Stand sideways to the ball, grip the stick with two hands at the top, so giving a forceful long lever (see Fig. 3).

Fig. 3. The grip for driving

Whilst the arms are swinging the stick forward, the hips rotate and the body weight is transferred from the back foot forward on to the front foot as the ball is struck. Be sure your head is over the ball, the face of the stick is flat against the ball at the moment of impact and that the swing follows through the line of the ball in the direction required. (See Fig. 4.)

Fig. 4. The drive (1); The drive (2); The drive (3)

In addition:

(a) A quick straight swing and a firm right hand at the moment of contact will impart speed to the ball. Some players visibly use their right hands to push through the swing in order to get greater power.

(b) A short back swing and follow-through will produce an efficient and effective stroke. Any swing tending to reach shoulder level is a technically poor stroke and liable to let you down at the crucial moment, so it is well worth the effort to remodel it.

PRACTICES

Individual

(1) Have two balls—hit one as hard as possible, the second, hit to travel half the distance. Aim—power hitting and an appreciation of the slower, more sympathetic pass ideal for hard and fast surfaces.

(2) Hit a ball along a straight line. Aim—to discover whether your preparation and swing are in a straight line resulting in an accurate shot or pass.

(3) Shooting practice. Arrange a number of balls around the edge of the circle. Start from either side, and move quickly from ball to ball aiming to knock over, alternately, the targets placed just inside both posts. Aim—accuracy, speed of the shot, moving quickly to the ball.

Groups

In threes (right wing, centre-forward and left inner). The right wing dribbles the ball and practises centring, for the centre-forward or left inner to control and shoot at goal. Both the 'centre' and shot should be hard, accurate and executed on the move.

(Reverse the practice for the left wing.)

THE PUSH

The push stroke is exactly as it describes itself—a thrusting away of the ball along the ground. Unlike the drive, there is no swing involved and the whole action is carried out with firm wrist, and a transference of body weight from foot to foot.

(1) Grip the stick in the same way as for dribbling and receiving.
(2) Position the ball at the side.
(3) Place your stick behind and touching the ball.
(4) Have your weight on the back foot.

Keep your head over the ball, move forward in a line on to the front foot, simultaneously thrusting the ball away—strong wrists add extra power. Follow through with the stick in the direction you want the ball to go. (Fig. 5.) Be sure that:

(a) there is no sound of contact between the stick and ball, and
(b) the ball is made to run along the ground.

Fig. 5. The push stroke as the arms begin their thrusting movement

This stroke's main asset is the disguise it offers to the player's intentions, for with no back lift, it is very difficult for the opposition to see and anticipate when it is going to happen. Practise this stroke until it is strong, flat, very accurate and quick in execution.

PRACTICES
Individual

(1) Line a number of balls across and a little way in front of you—move toward each ball, and without a sound of contact, push the ball forward. Aim—to develop resilient wrists 'feeling' the ball.
(2) Arrange a line of balls—push them alternately to the right and left. Aim—to appreciate the different relationship of the ball to the feet in both situations.
(3) Run, dribbling the ball, shoot at a target in the goal with a push stroke. Aim—a quick perfect execution.

THE FLICK

In order to clarify any confusion there might be over Flick strokes and Scoop strokes—I describe a Flick as a lifted push stroke, often spinning—and a Scoop stroke as one involving a 'digging' action which lifts the ball upwards either high into the air or over a stick.

Players seem to learn this tricky stroke more quickly on comparing and contrasting it with a push.

The similarities are:

Grip.

The thrusting movement.

No back lift as the movement starts with the stick behind the ball.

The need for strong wrists.

Good follow through.

In addition:

Position the ball in front of the front foot. Keep the weight on the back foot long enough to get under the ball before transferring the body weight on to the front foot. This gives the ball sufficient forward projection to make a long pass or shot. At the same time, a quick twisting or rotatory movement with the wrists will assist the flick to spin—a difficult shot for the goalkeeper to deal with. (See Fig. 6.)

Fig. 6. The flick stroke (1); The flick stroke (2)

The spin is the most difficult part of the stroke. Unlike bowling in cricket, when the fingers do the work, the flat face of the stick must obtain the spin. Try to maintain a contact with the stick on the ball as long as possible, 'feeling' first:

(1) the right side of the ball, then
(2) the underside,
(3) the left side, and
(4) ending with a final flick over with the toe of the stick. (A much easier knack with the old English-style stick.)

Once mastered, a spinning shot can be:

(1) Made to spin off the goalkeeper's pads,
(2) made to drop just in front of her pads, shooting off at a tangent as it lands,
(3) curved in flight.

All these are very tricky shots for a goalkeeper to save, putting her on the defensive and therefore unable to set up an attacking situation.

In defence—under extreme pressure the flick can be useful to lift the ball over the sticks of the opposition and place a long pass to your forwards. Do not put much spin on, for you may confuse your own team as well as the opposition.

PRACTICES

(1) Tie a rope or some bands across a goal mouth approximately 24 inches off the ground, stand at a distance and flick the balls over. With success, move farther away until you are making your shot from just inside the edge of the circle.

(2) On the move, dribble from the 25-yard line and flick over the target.

(3) Hang two ropes down from the cross bar in approximately the position the goalkeeper might be and aim your flick to the corners on either side. Remember, there is no limit to the height of the shot so long as you satisfy the umpire that, with your placement and control of the ball, you are in no way causing danger to the goalkeeper.

(4) *To practice spin*—Paint half the ball with a distinctive colour. Make your flick, noting the colour of the ball in flight. If the two colours still appear distinct, you are getting no spin. If the two colours merge, you are succeeding.

(5) From a point in the circle, flick a series of balls to drop a yard in front of the goal line; watch carefully to see if the ball moves either to the right or left or gathers momentum after striking the ground.

RECEIVING

Good receiving of the ball is one of the most important factors in attaining good stickwork. To achieve this, the ball should be controlled in the best position with a view to the next move. It is infuriating if the ball pops away from your stick and you have to re-position before dodging or passing. Any expert will quickly spot another in the ability to receive the ball well. Its advantages are obvious—immediate action.

In the early stages, receiving the ball is taught as the stop, and is an essential for a good corner taken at any level. In achieving a good stop, try catching a hard ball thrown at you. It will not be long before you realise the importance of 'giving a little' with your hands at the moment of impact.

To stop a ball coming towards you from in front:

(1) Grip the stick with the hands apart.
(2) Watch the oncoming ball very carefully.
(3) Position yourself behind the line of the ball and in the last movement, relax your wrists to 'give' the necessary amount to trap the ball, keeping your head well over it.

However, the ball is likely to come from five other directions:

(1) *from the right*—swerve towards it. Turn the stick to meet the ball, take it on your right side. (See plate 14.)
(2) *from the left*—again, do not wait for it to come to you, go to meet it with your stick again turned to face the ball. On making contact, re-position yourself behind the ball so that you are

Fig. 7. Receiving the ball from behind and on the right

ready for the next move. Passes coming from behind need much the same technique but with more twist of the body. In both cases, the feet continue to move forward.

(3) *from behind and on the right*—the upper part of the body twists around to the right so that the stick faces the ball and actually makes contact near your heels. The ball is then guided quickly forward to a comfortable and useful position. (Fig. 7.)

(4) *from behind and on the left*—the twist is not so great and it is possible to let the ball run forward, within your 'giving' action, to control it in a position ahead of you. (Fig. 8.)

Fig. 8. Receiving the ball from behind and on the left

(5) Unfortunately—some defence players always seem to pass the ball directly at the heels of their forwards—perhaps it is the forwards' fault for being particularly immobile. But there is an easy remedy, and that is for the forwards to position themselves at an angle to the person with the ball whilst waiting for their pass.

N.B. *Never wait for a ball if it is coming slowly, always go to meet it. And do 'show' where you want the ball, by holding your stick turned and ready, indicating the exact spot where you wish the ball to arrive*; this will give the defence a target to aim at and you the opportunity to receive an accurate pass.

TACKLING

The aim of the tackle is to rob an opponent of the ball, and is not successful unless the tackler has the ball under control and ready to use on the completion of the actual tackle. Since it is the ball which the tackler wants, it is this that she must watch most carefully, and time her tackle when the ball is farthest away from her opponent's stick. To do this, it is quite a helpful tip to try to gauge the rhythm of the opponent's dribbling action, and time the moment of tackling to coincide with the gap between the taps.

Forward Tackle. Grip the stick firmly with the hands apart and move towards your opponent with your stick on the ground, remembering to watch the ball. Position yourself on the ball side, keeping well balanced ready to move quickly in any direction. Now, either

(a) tackle by bringing your stick through the line of the ball and with the aid of strong pushing wrists cause your opponent to lose it to you, or

(b) 'rob' your opponent of the ball by pulling it out of the path of her stick. This move has to be quick, neat and expertly timed.

Tackle from the Right. Catch up with your opponent on her right side, grip your stick firmly and time pulling the ball towards you, getting your own feet out of the way quickly, ready to change direction to go the other way.

Tackle from the Left/Circular Tackle. The tackler is required to catch up with her opponent and before making the tackle, reach a position slightly ahead so that in taking the ball and moving across in front of her opponent, she does not cause any bodily contact or obstruction.

EMERGENCY TACKLES

Sometimes a player finds herself requiring extra reach to make a tackle; this can be helped by making the tackle one-handed.

Lunge Tackle. Approach your opponent on her right side, holding your stick in two hands. (See Plate 14.) If you are unable to reach the ball, extend your reach—i.e. let go with your right hand, and swing the stick round and down to meet the ball, intending to do one of three things:

(1) to deflect the ball away to her non-stick side for one of your team to clear,

(2) whilst she over-runs, to move behind her to collect the ball,

(3) to slow your opponent sufficiently for you to catch up and

place two hands on the stick, and continue as in tackling from the right.

Jab Tackle. This time the tackler is coming up on the left as for the circular tackle. Knowing that the opponent is out of normal range stretch your left arm, firmly gripping the top of the stick so that the blade is slanting upwards and contact the ball with the bottom edge of the stick, poking it across your opponent in order to retrieve the ball on the other side yourself, or for another member of your team to do so.

N.B. *Emergency tackles are the weakest way to foil an attack and can never substitute a two-handed attempt. When in use, always endeavour to get the second hand back on the stick at the earliest opportunity.*

Rules concerning Tackling:

(1) You may not play or obstruct the stick of your opponent in any way.

(2) You may not run between your opponent and the ball or interpose yourself or your stick as an obstruction.

(3) You may not put the ball between your feet.

(4) You may not trip, shove, charge, strike at, or in any way personally handle your opponent.

In Conclusion:
A good tackler is not drawn by an opposing forward into making a tackle, but is a player who either:

calmly takes the initiative and moves when the moment is opportune neatly to take the ball, or by hovering, forces the forward into taking the initiative, relying on a good eye to spot her intention, and a quick reaction to win the ball.

On some occasions, a threatened tackle will force the player to pass hurriedly, so that another member of the defence can intercept the ball.

PRACTICES
In all practice sessions:

(1) Position a third person ready for the pass and insist that the tackler, having gained possession of the ball, passes to her accurately. Sometimes a target would be a satisfactory substitute.

(2) For learning purposes—progress the speed from walking pace to top speed, ensuring that no rules are infringed.

(3) Top speed is essential for the final achievement.

Individual practices are best geared to strengthening the left arm and watching the ball most carefully.

Suggestion—Regularly hold a tennis ball in the left hand and squeeze it a certain number of times, or use any other exercise with the same basis. Deliberately use your left hand more for sporting activities. Practise moving the ball with only the left hand on the stick.

Training a quick eye can be done in various ways:

Working with a tennis or rubber ball on a wall.

Squash is a wonderful game for quickening reaction and training the eye.

BEATING AN OPPONENT

This can be done in two ways:

1. *With the help of another member of the team by*

(a) a timely pass to a player better positioned than yourself;

(b) combining with another team member to outwit the opponent. In this particular case, *the triangular pass* is useful. For example:

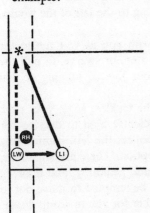

Fig. 9. The triangular pass

Supposing a left wing is having difficulty in using the forward space ahead of her owing to the good positioning of opposing right half. If the left inner is positioned alongside, approximately five yards distant, it would be possible for the left wing to dribble toward the right half and at the last minute slip a pass square to her left inner who returns the ball quickly into the forward space on the non-stick side of the right half. The success of this plan depends upon two things

(i) The ability of the left wing to disguise her intention.
(ii) The speed with which the left inner can receive and pass the ball accurately forward.

2. *With an individual effort:*

(a) By getting to the ball first.
(b) By a quick change of speed, either acceleration or deceleration.
(c) Dodging an opponent.

DODGING

When in possession of the ball, to beat an opponent by an individual effort and still have the ball under close control constitutes a successful dodge.

Method 1. Right Dodge. Part company with the ball by pushing it to the right, whilst swerving and passing to the left of the would-be tackler. Collect the ball behind her.

Method 2. Left Dodge. Keep the ball with you as you run to the left of your opponent, timing your side step, or swerve, to pull the ball away from the tackler. Resume your line of running or you may veer too much to the left.

Method 3. Scoop Dodge. On meeting the tackler, angle your stick to lift the ball over her stick just sufficiently high to deceive her eye, and just far enough to be able to collect the ball comfortably on the other side with no fear of interception. There are situations, particularly near the circle, when by 'back pedalling' and drawing the ball towards you, the defender may be tempted to move out to challenge, leaving enough space behind her for you to scoop dodge.

Method 4. Reverse Dodge. Reverse the stick, tap or pull the ball to the right, taking care not to obstruct the would-be tackler by getting your shoulder and/or body between her and the ball. Accelerate, run wide and so long as it is necessary to avoid obstruction, dribble the ball on your left.

ESSENTIALS

Keep the ball as close to your stick as possible and watch the opposition carefully for the right moment to make the avoiding action. The choice of dodge will depend upon the whereabouts of the space—on the whole, the right side of the field tends to have more success with the right dodge—and the left side more success with the left dodge, as both actions take the ball away from the often crowded centre of the field.

Make your task easier by wrong-footing your opponent—lead her to believe you intend one method so that her weight begins to move over, and surprise her with another. In catching the waiting defence player off balance, the player will find it much easier to dodge and take up less space in doing so.

The timing of the actual dodge is critical—watch the closing gap between the ball, your opponent and her stick, assessing the relative speeds and watching for the moment of challenge. At this, take prompt action, and if necessary swerve to avoid body contact. Having successfully rounded the obstacle, taking as little space as possible, maintain the ball under close control ready for the next move.

Forwards do find it more difficult to dodge, in that, any movement whilst running at top speed requires more skill in its execution. Therefore, when practising it is helpful to a forward to pay particular attention to the wrong-footing movement immediate to the actual dodge. The 'hovering' back can present more problems than a 'challenging' back, because it is the forward who must take the initiative in timing her dodge, and use quick acceleration, causing the defender to mistime her tackle.

An almost stationary dodge to avoid a fast incoming opponent should be delayed until the last moment to give as little indication as possible as to the dodger's intention. Otherwise, it may be possible for the opponent to swerve and regain the ball.

PRACTICES
Individually

(1) Stand astride, put the ball in front of the right foot, pull it across in front of the left foot and return it to starting position

by working the left wrist particularly so that it is not necessary to turn the stick over. Progress through walking to running, still 'working the ball'.

(2) The ball follows the same path as No. 1, but, to bring the ball back to the starting position, reverse the stick and draw the ball back.

(3) Arrange obstacles to swerve round and practise parting with the ball and collecting it on the other side.

(4) Practise running and scooping over the lines of the hockey field.

In practising dodging another player, arrange a secondary task to ensure that the dodger has retained sufficient control of the ball to use it advantageously, i.e:

(1) Shoot at goal. Use the circle and the goal. Arrange three or four players, starting from the back line, to follow each other round the circle edge reasonably spaced. The first of a group of waiting players dribbles a ball from the same point on the opposite side around the edge of the circle to meet and dodge, in turn, the three oncoming opponents. At any given moment, the dodger must quickly gather the ball to shoot. The goalkeeper should practise her positioning by moving around her goal area to cover all the possible angles of the shot. The practice is continuous, but should be reversed to hit both to the right and to the left.

(2) Pass to another player. Practise in threes. A forward chases a long ball which is intercepted by a member of the defence who clears accurately to her own forward waiting a distance away. In clearing to the right, quick footwork to get the feet round the ball is essential for a quick clearance.

REVERSE STICK

The weaker side of a hockey player is her left side, because the stick is designed with the right-hander's natural movement in mind. The left side of the body is generally referred to as non-stick side, and in order to play the ball on that side, the stick must be 'reversed'. That is, turned so that the toe of the stick is nearer to you. The reversing can be done in two different ways—by turning the toe of the stick over or by dropping the toe of the stick. I favour the latter. It accentuates the importance of the left arm and is more consistent with the teaching of general technique as well as reverse stick skills. For instance, although it matters little which way you turn your stick to reverse hit, it makes quite a difference to playing the other skills comfortably and quickly. Try controlling a ball that has come across from your right and is too far ahead to play with both hands, by extending the left forearm and letting the toe of the stick drop under—it is a much quicker and more natural movement. In using the other method to reverse stick dodge, and having drawn the ball to the right, a further wristy movement is necessary before it is possible to dribble or hit the ball.

In order to play the ball competently on the reverse stick side, it is necessary to change the grip. Allow the stick to swivel in the left hand and adjust the right hand to a comfortable position, keep the hands slightly apart—more so for movements requiring strength, i.e. dodging, fielding, tackling, etc. (Fig. 10).

Fig. 10. Using the stick reversed to draw the ball across the body to the right

The first object should be to familiarise yourself with the change of grip.

(1) Practise pulling the ball from side to side in front of you.

(2) With your feet running along a line, dribble the ball, continually moving it from one side of the line to the other—reversing the stick to bring the ball back from the left each time.

Now combine the footwork with the reverse stick.

(1) Practise a series of sharp taps to the right interspersed with a short dribble. The running track is in right angles.

(2) Combine with a partner. Run with a partner alongside approximately three yards distant—adapt the right-angled tap to a hit, concentrating on keeping the head over the ball so that the heel of the stick contacts the ball.

By now you should be ready to progress to the individual skills and as you do so beware of the danger of obstruction by interposing your own body between your opponent and the ball.

Reverse stick dodge   With a swift movement, draw the ball to the right and, giving your opponent a wide berth, dribble the ball around her non-stick side, taking care not to put your body between her and the ball. To lessen the chance of obstruction keep the ball well in front of you, and as you pass your opponent, play the ball on your left side with the reverse stick. Resume a normal dribbling position once clear of your opponent.

PRACTICES

(1) In an astride standing position, practise drawing the ball from side to side so that it moves parallel with the toes but well in front of the body. Concentrate on keeping an effective grip on the stick even though it is constantly changing as you move the ball first to the right then to the left. Progress to moving forward.

(2) Individually practise dribbling the ball on the reverse stick side, taking care not to exaggerate the turning in of the right shoulder, and then tap the ball smartly into a comfortable dribbling position.

(3) Combine the two previous movements, concentrating on making the ball travel a right-angled path. Add a static then moving opponent.

Reverse stick hit   Keep your head over the ball and, with a short back lift, hit the ball firmly to the right. More power will be obtained by hitting the ball with the heel of the stick and using the right hand to 'sweep' the ball across the body, finishing with a strong follow-through in the direction of the departing ball. Practise hitting off either foot.

PRACTICES

(1) In fours, with the ball moving anti-clockwise, reverse stick hit, stop and reverse stick hit etc., making the movement strong, quick and accurate.

(2) Dribble the ball at top speed, and aim to hit target, i.e. tin, basket, etc., using the reverse stick.

(3) Left inner dribbles the ball toward the near goal post to draw

the goalkeeper, then suddenly hits the ball with a reversed stick across the goal mouth for an adjacent forward to put neatly into the net on the goalkeeper's non-stick side.

(4) Any game situation requiring a sudden square pass, i.e. left wing centring off the back line.

Reverse stick stop Having stopped the ball on the non-stick side with the stick reversed, it is a very awkward position from which to play the ball, so it is necessary to correct the ball's position as quickly as possible either by drawing the ball back into a playable position in front of yourself, or, rapidly moving the feet round to the left side of the ball.

This technique should never be used as a substitute for quick footwork—its accomplishment is to increase your range of intercepting and is particularly useful to defence players.

One-handed reversed stick In order to field a ball that is just out of reach on the non-stick side, reverse the stick and stretch your left arm, aiming to gather the ball and move it into a stronger position.

Practise as a left wing. Chase a cross pass that is just too far ahead and about to go off the side line, and by running at top speed and reaching forward with a reversed stick, keep the ball in the field of play. Having practised this several times you will appreciate the importance of a strong left wrist.

Centre-halves also find this technique most useful in helping to intercept the cross pass.

E42, 685.

2 Defence Play

DEFENCE PLAY

As attacking ideas have developed, so a defensive system has been evolved to offset the forwards' schemes. Already teams are trying new formations in an effort to shake the game from its orthodoxy. However, it is as well to weave new tactics around a basic covering system.

COVERING

Briefly, the orthodox defensive system is arranged to provide as many lines of defence in the face of attack as practical. Goalkeeping is dealt with in Chapter 4, so I will begin with the two backs—and the golden rule for these two is never to stand square (i.e. on the same line sideways across the field). If you do the forwards will be through you in a flash. You will be expected to combine by positioning yourselves to cover for each other. On whichever side the attack develops against you, that particular back should be prepared to tackle the inner in possession of the ball, whilst the other moves quickly round and behind to cover her 'partner'. Should the ball be passed to the other inner, then a quick re-positioning of the covering back into the tackle is necessary and the original tackler must move smartly into the covering position. (Fig. 11.)

The covering should be approximately in a position in line with the ball and the goal. However, a thoughtless back can often unsight the goalkeeper and it is as well to position yourself slightly off centre toward your side of the field, but ready to move quickly either to the right or left. When covering in circle play where space is minimal, there is a real problem of unsighting your goalkeeper, and a useful tip to remember, when moving to cover, is to glance over your shoulder—if you can see her all is well, but, if you cannot, you are probably plumb in front. Encourage your goalkeeper to call to you—that will soon sort you out. If she is also confident to call "mine" on shots she wishes to deal with, you will know what to leave and what to take. This is a necessity for good relations with your goalkeeper.

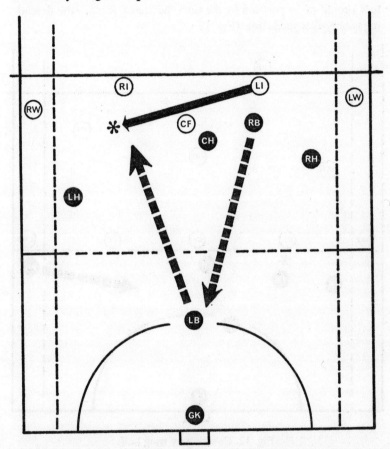

Fig. 11. Covering. The covering back is the L.B. The moment the opposing L.I. passes across towards the R.I., the L.B. moves out to challenge whilst the R.B. moves in to cover

Now the immediate consequence of covering backs is to leave an inside forward unmarked. In mid-field do not worry, but in the circle it is essential that the inside forward is marked closely and that will be the task of the wing half *farthest away from the ball*.

Obviously the inner is more dangerous than the wing, being nearer the ball, and if a forward has to be left unmarked, it is usually best to leave the wing. At what moment the wing half moves on to the inner is always a point for discussion. I believe firmly that the wing half should be in position by the time the attack reaches the defending twenty-five yards line. (Fig. 12.)

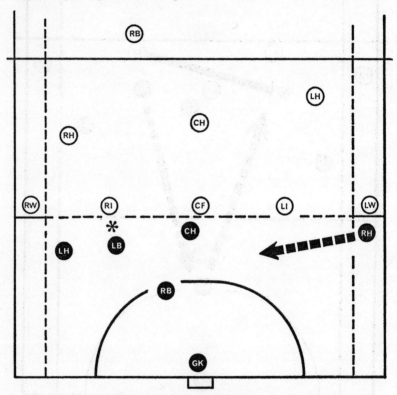

Fig. 12. Covering by wing half

The remaining defence players have straightforward tasks. The centre-half accounts for the centre-forward, and the half on the ball-side of the field will be doing one of two things; either, having been passed, catching up in order to make a tackle, or, marking the space between the inner and wing.

The half-back line must also provide depth in covering and this will depend on:

(1) The area of attack.

(2) The position of the backs.

Consider Point 1

Covering by the wing halves, if the attack is through the centre (Fig. 13).

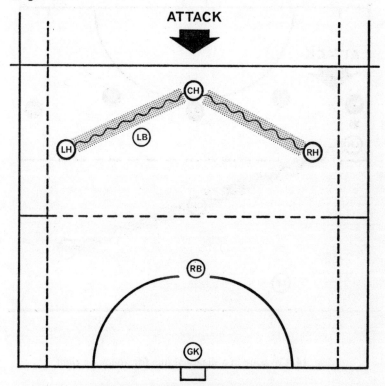

Fig. 13. Covering attack through centre

Covering in a diagonal line if the attack is on the right (Fig. 14). In this case, note the slightly deeper covering of the right half. Both the right back and the right half should always remember to cover slightly more deeply because any play on their non-stick side demands a longer run round, in order to make a tackle.

Consider Point 2 *Playing Square*

Never be caught standing side by side with another defence player for it requires only one simple through pass placed between you for you both to be beaten. One player positioned a few feet in front of the other is all that is needed to cover the centre space, for the rear player will have that split second longer to see and cope with the pass.

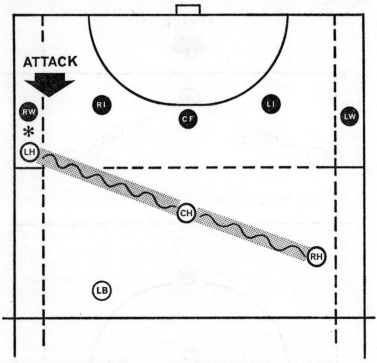

Fig. 14. Covering in a diagonal line for attack on right

A defence system must be thoroughly INTEGRATED and prepared to meet all possibilities—remember the story of the spider and the fly, and weave a cobweb on which the opposing forwards will be trapped. When the opposing attack develops, speedy mobility in re-grouping may be required to stem the forward movement, and in these situations a quick-thinking, calm co-operation within the system is vital. No system is infallible; it may break down owing to the sheer individual brilliance of the forward in possession, or per-haps the left back is drawn out of the covering position before the right back has moved round to take her place. Whatever the situation, a well-organised defence will have the answer to most situations and combine to act swiftly on its own initiative to cope with the surprises.

Some forward lines deliberately set out to confuse and tire the defence by interchanging and until an inexperienced defence finds the answer, this can be a most successful tactic. To outwit this tactic, alter the idea of marking the player to *marking the channel*, so that if the space used by the five forwards is divided into five channels the members of the defence mark their channel or zone

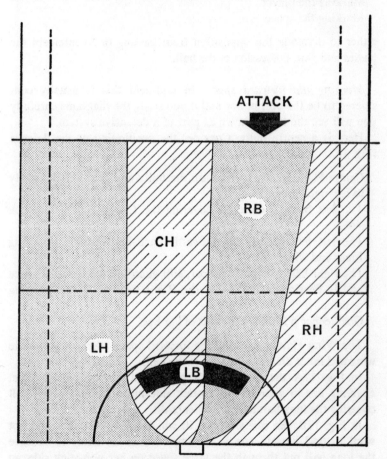

Fig. 15. The zone areas when attack is on the right. Adapt same principle for coping with the attack on the left

and take responsibility for any player who moves into it. Should the forwards tend to crowd, they will be playing into your 'net', for you could mark more than one player at a time (Fig. 15).

MARKING

The basic objective is to limit your opponent's activities, and is achieved as part of the system in two ways:

Marking the player
Marking the space

either to dissuade the opposition from passing or to intercept the passes and gain possession of the ball.

Marking the forward space. In mid-field this is usually considered to be the best policy and if you study the diagrams carefully you will see the tactic shown as part of a defensive system.

Here is a centre bully. Consider the positioning of the defence (Fig. 16).

Centre-Half. Ready to back up the bully and positioned slightly to her right because—
The left back is close by covering the Centre-Half's non-stick side.
The left half guards the forward space between the opposing Inner and wing.
The right half is slightly deeper, still guarding the forward space and is bearing in mind that the Right Back is in the covering position.
Goalkeeper positioned in front of her line.

The Wing Halves marking the forward space when the opposite wing and inner are in possession of the ball.

In Fig. 17A the Left Half is positioned nearer the side line, enabling her to guard her non-stick side more closely, whilst still covering the long ball on her 'easier' side.

In Fig. 17B, the one situation in which the Right Half does not want to find herself, she is chasing back in an effort to retrieve the long ball put through the large space on her non-stick side, so she has positioned herself to block the forward space at roughly the point of a triangle between the two opposition.

Plate 1 (*Left*). Goalkeeper guarding on goalpost semi-circle. Completely blocking any shot from an acute angle. Note how the pad overlaps the goalpost.

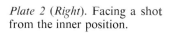

Plate 2 (*Right*). Facing a shot from the inner position.

Plate 3 (*Left*). The shot from the C.F. at the edge of the circle leaves the goalkeeper with the most ground to cover sideways.

Plate 4 (Right). With weight well forward on her toes the goalkeeper 'knees' a high shot bringing it safely down and into a good position for a clearance.

Plate 5 (Left). A goalkeeper well poised at the moment of contact can easily sweep the ball away from an opponent's stick.

Plate 6 (Right). Stopping a shot with the stick. Notice the added strength of the stick braced against the forearm. Stick stops should only be used in an emergency when it is impossible to reach the ball with a foot.

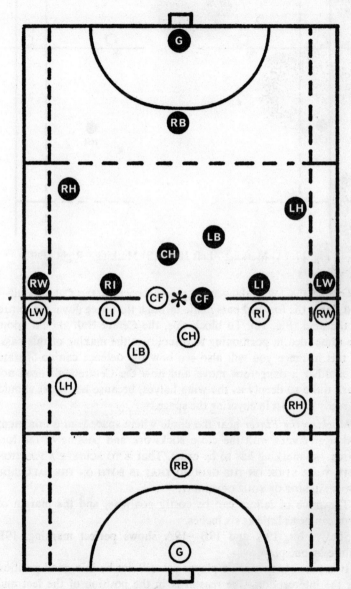

Fig. 16. Centre bully. Positioning of defence

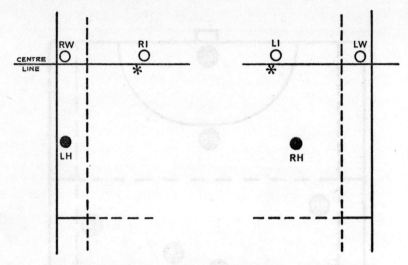

Fig. 17. (A) Marking—Left Half; (B) Marking—Right Half

One of the really dangerous passes concerns the Centre-Half—and this is the forward pass made through the space down the centre of the field (Fig. 18). To block this, the Centre-Half should adopt the same idea in positioning to discourage the making of this pass. In this instance you will also see how the defence can co-operate to smother a dangerous move and how the Centre-Half need not mark quite so deeply as the wing halves, because her backs should be ready to assist in covering the space.

Marking the Player near the circle where space is at a minimum —danger comes with the close stickwork and passing of the forwards—so marking has to be exact. That is TO ACHIEVE A POSITION WITH YOUR STICK ON THE GROUND THAT IS BOTH ON THE BALL SIDE AND GOAL SIDE OF YOUR OPPONENT.

The price of failure can be costly goalwise, and the margin of error can be as little as six inches.

Study Figs. 19A and 19B—19A shows perfect marking, 19B failure by one player.

It is possible to mark a player yet still not be in a good position for the interception—the reason is in the position of the feet and the amount of turn to face the person with the ball. A good marker will be on the ball side and the goal side of her opponent positioned

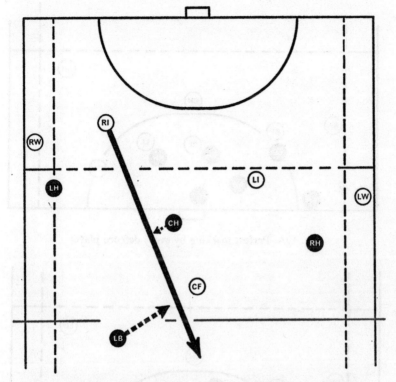

Fig. 18. Blocking the forward pass made through the space down the centre of the field

ready, anticipating the move forward up the field for the interception.

Negative Play. There are situations in which a defence player is wise not to commit herself. A forward in controlled possession of the ball is a dangerous person to challenge. Force her to take the initiative by hovering and be ready to pounce the moment she gives some indication of her intention. Remember, the more defence players the opposing forward line can eliminate, the greater the space in which to work in the shooting area, so they will be deliberately tempting you to commit yourself.

Positive Play. To take the initiative—move in to intercept or tackle, and follow with a constructive pass. This will require exact timing, for a player moving forward is an easy person to dodge. Do

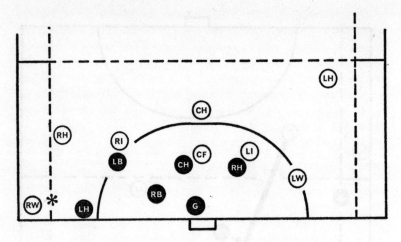

Fig. 19A. Perfect marking by every defence player

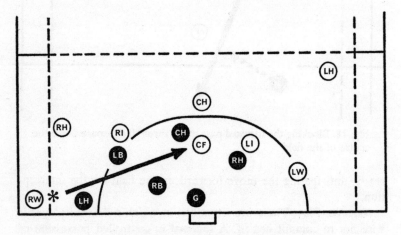

Fig. 19B. C.H. fails to mark correctly

not commit yourself unless you are sure of success, but once sure, move quickly and confidently and having achieved possession of the ball, do not delay in using it wisely. *A defence player should never be caught in possession.*

Rather than take individual positions, I propose to enlarge on the attributes that go to make the ideal defensive player, believing that every player should be equipped to play any situation.

(1) Anticipation. This is the correct interpretation of various signs and signals to forestall the opponents' intention with a spoiling move of your own, in order to gain the ball and get your own team to attack, Some players aid their anticipation by trying to put themselves into their opponents' shoes to see the immediate situation as the opponents see it. There are many aids to anticipation —the more you play hockey the more you will notice. Little individual things, such as:

(a) a forward about to shoot gives away the intended direction by lifting her head to take aim.
(b) a left wing chassé steps, indicating the intending cross pass.

Anticipation requires a vital sense of timing to put the operation into effect at the right moment, and a physical ability to achieve possession of the ball.

(2) Good Timing. The obvious reference here is in tackling and dodging. (At this point it might be well to remind yourselves of the techniques, in which case, refer back to pages 13 and 17.) Good timing is the hallmark of the class player—i.e. the type of player who performs her skills with extreme ease, and apparently in plenty of time. It is an art which is difficult to coach—the best you can do is to eliminate any bad points in technique, train acute observation and build confidence.

(3) Good Ball Control is even more vital for defence players, for one error can be disastrous. The stopping or controlling should be achieved in the position most convenient for your next move— for instance, a decision whether you intend passing the ball to your left or right makes quite a difference in the stopping and positioning of the ball in the first place. When under pressure, the slightest bounce forward off your stick could be snapped up by an oncoming forward and you would have no second chance. Another situation comes to mind, again under pressure—the ball is just running loose ahead of a fast-moving forward—a swift decision is called for; have you time to move in and rob her of the ball, using a stop followed by a hit to your attack, or must you deflect it from her path, follow it and then use it constructively? Intercepting is the other occasion for demonstrating good ball control—frequently in a game, a player may show good powers of anticipation, only to see her efforts to intercept fail as a result of missing the ball or allowing it to bounce off her stick back to the other team. The secret lies in learning to

watch the ball very closely—not many of us can honestly say that we watch the ball actually make contact with our sticks—often, we give up looking when the ball is about twelve inches away, and you should know that anything can happen in those twelve inches, particularly on a bumpy pitch. Therefore, train yourselves to *watch* the ball intently. (Playing tennis will help.) Couple this with a sensitivity in your wrists (the tighter you grip your stick, the more the ball will ricochet), hold your stick firmly, yet with a relaxed grip, and at the moment of impact 'give' with the ball, the degree will depend on the speed of the ball meeting the stick, and this experience you must discover for yourselves. Finally, your balance and good footwork could make the difference between success and disaster. In trying to keep your head more or less over the ball, you should be in a balanced position ready to move in any direction.

(4) Good Interception demands:

   (a) Anticipation.
   (b) Split-second timing.
   (c) Good ball control plus quick acceleration.

Every player should be adept at getting off the mark quickly, with the stick on the ground. Ask a friend to hit balls across the field to a third person enabling you to practise sprinting to intercept, keep the ball in close control and make your pass to a member of your own team waiting up-field. Interceptions are possible at corners, and it can be a real challenge to see whether you can be first out and achieve possession of the ball.

(5) Intelligence. In determining our ideal defence player, it will not be long before somebody suggests that intelligence might have something to do with it. What an understatement! A thinking brain coupled with a co-operative body is the criterion of our shining example.

Schemes to outwit the opposition even when under extreme pressure are an asset to any team. To aid my own concentration, I try to be one move ahead of the opposition—this 'mind reading' act can be developed by:

   (1) Learning to play on the forward line and discovering for yourself the various positional opportunities.
   (2) Reading and listening to coaching points concerning all other positions.
   (3) Combining cunning with skill and putting into practice.

(6) 'Unflappability'. It is essential that a defence player should never panic or at least never give the appearance of agitation. Give the impression that you have every situation firmly in hand.

(7) Stamina. Fitness is the key to success. (See page 102.)

THE CO-OPERATION OF BACKS AND HALF BACKS IN ATTACK AND DEFENCE

The Backs

Consider your play as a partnership with the position of the ball as of prime importance. The degree of co-operation should be one hundred per cent.

Consider this situation:

(1) Following a cross pass from the opposing Right Back, the defending and covering Right Back immediately dashes forward in an effort to reach the ball before the opposing Left Inner, with no thought to the relative position of her partner the Left Back (Fig. 20).

(2) The Left Inner, alive to the situation, has made very sure that she gains possession of the ball first, and immediately catches the two backs at their most vulnerable moment by passing the ball down through the centre space for her Centre Forward to run on to (Fig. 21).

Now consider the situation with a co-operative and intelligent Right Back who is aware of the danger:

(3) Seeing the opposing Right Back passing the ball into the space ahead of the Left Inner, and knowing there is a possibility of being beaten to the ball—she begins her move into the attack having made sure that her partner, the Left Back, is rapidly coming back to cover and is past the moment of 'squareness'. (Fig. 22.) The next move will depend upon the initiative of the Left Inner, bearing in mind that none of the defence has yet been eliminated.

Circle Play: Another situation requiring a quick re-organisation is in *coping with a clever cross pass to the player farthest from the ball.* On page 38 I give two suggestions for this.

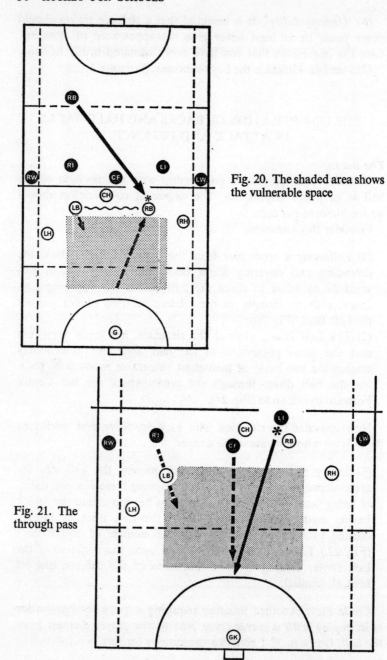

Fig. 20. The shaded area shows
the vulnerable space

Fig. 21. The
through pass

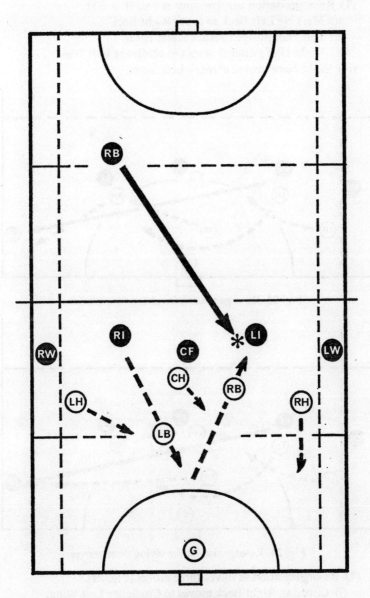

Fig. 22. Co-operation

(1) Re-organisation involves four moves (Fig. 23).
  (i) Marking Left Back to cover Right Back.
  (ii) Left Half moves to mark Right Inner.
  (iii) Right Half switches across to challenge Left Wing.
  (iv) Right Back moves to mark Left Inner.

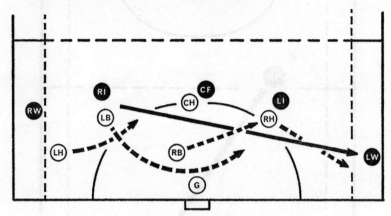

Fig. 23. Re-organisation involving four moves

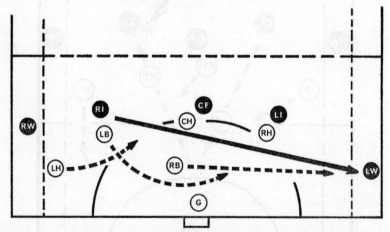

Fig. 24. Re-organisation involving three moves

(2) Re-organisation involves three moves (Fig. 24).
  (i) Covering Right Back moves to Challenge Left Wing.
  (ii) Left Back moves to cover Right Back.
  (iii) Left Half switches to mark Right Inner.

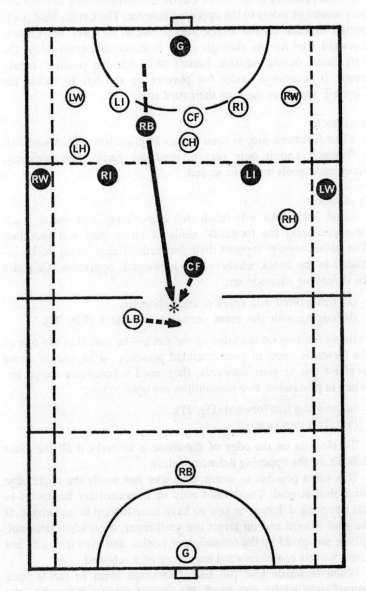

Fig. 25. The breakaway

The Breakaway (Fig. 25): A Centre-Forward waiting up-field can be a source of worry to the opposing defence. The Centre-Half is expected to back up the attack and is bound to leave her Centre-Forward free for the through pass; to cover this eventuality, the Left Back should position herself to tackle the possible breakaway. It is always easier for players on the left to tackle the Centre-Forward as she is on their stick side.

Half Backs

Their functions are, as their names implies, half a back and half a forward; and if only players used the name conscientiously, many more goals would be scored.

In Attack:

Good half-backs will relish this opportunity and spend much time practising the forwards' skills of circle play and shooting. The halves should support their forwards closely, ready to be included in the attack whenever the moment is opportune. Consider the defending situation on:

(a) being faced with seven or eight shooters,

(b) coping with the extra variations in attack (Fig. 26).

In positioning on the edge of the circle—be sure that the rest of the forwards know of your intended presence—a haphazard sortie is of no use to your forwards, they need a consistent supporter. When in possession, two possibilities are open to you:

(a) pass to a free forward (Fig. 27).

(b) take a shot yourself.

To close in on the edge of the circle is to make it all the more difficult for the opposing defence to clear.

It is often possible to worm your way just inside the circle edge for a shot at goal. There need only be a momentary hesitation in the opposing defence for you to have time to step in and shoot. If the shot is hard and on target the goalkeeper, more often than not, will be unsighted by the confusion of bodies, and even if you do not score, a lively centre-forward may score off a rebound.

When forwards lose the ball, encourage them to tackle back immediately whilst you block the escape routes; meanwhile the wing half farther from the ball should drop a little deeper to prepare to cover in the event of a breakaway.

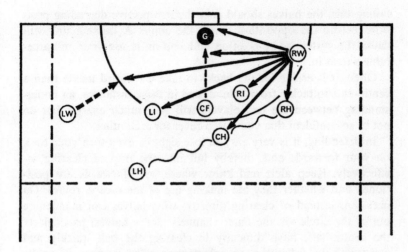

Fig. 26. The half-backs in attack

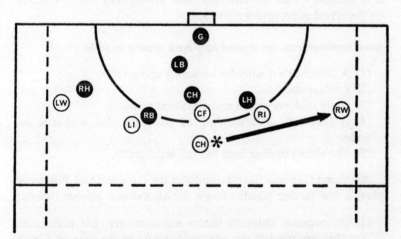

Fig. 27. Near the circle the wing is often left unguarded

In Defence:

Following a breakaway, the half-backs must re-position in the
defensive system as fast as they possibly can. Thus, if the halves
are faster than the forwards, it is to their great advantage. To regain the ball on a tackle back or interception is the first aim,

failing this, the halves should gain their respective defending positions before the opposition enters the circle. A missing link will cause the system to re-position and you must use your resourcefulness to fit in.

Often, it is easier for the backs to take a forward tackle than a centre-half to tackle from behind, and in these instances, an understanding between the two players will save much energy, but do not be so confident that you fail to cover for each other.

In defending, it is very easy to lose sight or even turn your back on your forwards and, thereby fall into the trap of clearing ineffectively. Keep alert and know where your forwards are positioned and whether they are making use of the escape routes. On occasion, instead of clearing directly, wing halves can manoeuvre out of the circle via the outer channels. Some halves, particularly the centre-half, have difficulty in clearing the ball quickly and constructively following an interception. The answer is to be found in their footwork—for a player to turn defence into attack, it is necessary that her feet and body are turning into the attack on the actual intercepting movement.

Basic requirements for a good half-back should include:

(1) A terrier-like quality for harassing opponents.
(2) Endless stamina.
(3) Good stickwork even under extreme pressure.
(4) A thorough understanding of positonal play within a defence.
(5) The ability to distribute the ball intelligently.

Assuming that you have assimilated the Covering and Positional play, a few further points remain for all defence players, briefly:

(1) On occasion delaying tactics are necessary, but make sure that they are not left too late, particularly in the case of a back delaying her forward tackle and finding herself forced to tackle in the circle. There, a mistake could lead to a penalty corner or even a goal.
(2) At all costs avoid giving away corners.
(3) Never retreat on your own goalkeeper or obscure her view.
(4) Clear quickly and accurately and never be caught in possession.

(5) Train yourself to be quick to turn and tackle back, generally harry your opponent and above all, never give up.

(6) Govern the depth of your backing up by comparing your speed with that of your opponent.

(7) Keep your stick close to the ground ready for all eventualities.

(8) LAST LINE OF DEFENCE. In a real emergency the covering wing-half should move in behind the goalkeeper. Avoid getting in her way and only take this extreme measure if you feel that you can save the ball from going over the goal line.

PRACTISE:

1. Quick acceleration, particularly coming out from a corner.
2. Accurate passing.
3. Fielding and controlling the ball from all angles.
4. Moving in all directions with your stick ready grazing the ground.
5. Dodging and tackling.
6. Pivotting and hitting quickly to the right, keeping the back lift short.
7. The movement of intercepting, controlling and passing the ball.
8. Emergency strokes, i.e. jab lunge.
9. Free hits (see page 83).
10. SHOOTING!

3 Forward Play

Forwards must score goals and to do this they must acquire skill, stamina and cunning. These are not easily acquired, and many hours of concentrated effort at all aspects are necessary to attain a good standard. Although individual positions differ, there is much in common.

First acquire a thorough understanding of the orthodox system of defence play. In fact, go so far as to play in the defence and get some experience from the other point of view—you will be amazed at the number of useful tips you will discover, not only concerning forwards but some of the problems of playing defence.

Not all defences play to the orthodox system, indeed, some seem to have no system at all, and in these instances it is vital that you should develop your ideas according to what lies ahead. It increases your chances of success to have a quick glance at the positioning of the opposition before you receive the ball.

Never be afraid to go alone for goal—but do not do it too often. Use the individual effort as an *element of surprise*.

Make it possible for your defence to use free hits advantageously by either *creating a space* for yourself or for another member of the team. When the opposition has free hits, make the conditions as difficult as possible. I suggest ringing the player in possession. (Refer to 'Hit outs', page 83.)

Distribute the ball sympathetically—Inside forwards who 'belt' the ball forward for the wings, with no thought to the relative speeds of the ball, the player and the best angle, are a menace. Sometimes consideration toward a tiring player is prudent.

Tackling back can sap a lot of energy—but it will help your defence tremendously if, on losing the ball, you train yourself to turn quickly and immediately set about winning it back. Therefore, practise both your circular tackle and left-hand lunge tackle as well as the footwork of a quick change of direction. And this brings me on to the subject of

Plate 7. The Opening Parade of the International Federation of Women's Hockey Associations' Conference and Tournament held at Leverkusen, Germany, 1967.

Plate 8 (*Above*). The short roll (*J. Braham, England to V. Robinson, England*). With so many opponents, this is a difficult moment for the attack. Instead of passing to the R.W., the R.H. rolls quickly to the R.I. who initiates the interchange by moving towards the ball and the side line.

Plate 9 (*Below*). The long roll from the defending area (*C. Aspinwall, England to P. Donaldson, England*). The ball is being rolled close to the line and with some force so that it gets to the Wing before the Half can intercept. Notice that the Wing is moving quickly towards the side line with her stick ready to trap the ball. Notice too that the L.B. has made herself available for a short roll.

Fitness—to be of real value to your team you must make every effort to have more than sufficient stamina for a match. The first sign of fatigue is a slackening in accuracy, something a forward cannot afford. (Fitness—see page 102.)

RUSHING THE GOALKEEPER

A forward who fails to rush and worry the goalkeeper is wasting a grand opportunity to score. As the shot is being made, dart to the goal mouth, with your stick on the ground, and try to contact the ball *either* to deflect it around her pads or to take the ricochet off her pads and flick the ball into the goal. If you:

(1) move or wait on a line with the player who has the ball, or
(2) keep on a line with the third defence and go for goal the moment the ball is hit, you cannot be offside.

Note rule 11 very carefully:

A player is offside if she is nearer her 'opponent's goal line than the striker or roller-in *at the moment when the ball is hit or rolled in* unless she is in her own half of the field or there are at least three of her opponents nearer to their own goal line than she is. A player who is in an offside position shall not be put onside by reason of the ball having touched or glanced off the stick or person of an opponent. She should not be penalised unless she is gaining an advantage from being or having been in an offside position'.

All players should be thoroughly conversant with this rule—particularly the centre-forward, who is often the spearhead of an attack and is in the best position for much close work. My tip for a nippy and goal-hunting forward is to watch the shooter very closely for some intimation of the direction of the shot and get to that point quickly, with the stick ready to pick up a clearance.

Give the goalkeeper no moment to clear the ball; the shooter must follow up quickly together with one or two other players close at hand, the remainder should wait momentarily to see the developments before adding their numbers. At this moment, the half-back line should be waiting like vultures near the edge of the circle to pounce on any stray balls.

Rushing the goalkeeper at a corner is easier, for once having seen the angle and knowing that the ball is not coming to you, start your run in to a point approximately halfway into the circle, pause slightly if you are a quick mover otherwise you may be caught off-side, note the intended direction of the shot, and as it is made, rush into the goal mouth ready to score off any rebound. Some players are so quick they can deflect the ball off the original course into the exact opposite side of the goal.

KEEP WELL SPACED

Crowding each other is often a fault with forwards. It usually stems from an anxiety to help, but it is a completely misguided effort—the closer you get, the easier it is for one defence player to mark two forwards. If an interchange seems probable, make it both prompt and purposeful.

SHOOTING

'A miss is as good as a mile' and it is well to remember that games are never won on misses. Therefore acquire the attributes of accuracy and cunning, together with a prompt execution. It should be obvious that hours of practice are involved to achieve this end.

Start shooting as an art as near the beginning of a hockey career as possible—goalkeepers are just as anxious to keep the goals out as you are to get them in.

(1) Practise from all points of the circle (you never know the angle from which you may get the opportunity to shoot).

(2) Practise the 'Whack' of a very hard drive.

(3) Practise the flick, the push, the scoop over the goalkeeper's head.

(4) Practise close-in work—the shot round the goalkeeper's pads.

(5) Create space in the goal, draw the goalkeeper to her right and then shoot to her non-stick side.

(6) Rushing is an art in itself and has already been mentioned.

Remember, whenever you are shooting against a goalkeeper, you will have to outwit or out-manoeuvre her, or beat her on a direct shot. If there is time, wrap up your intending method with another idea in an effort to wrong-foot her before placing the final shot.

An occasional solo effort is great fun to perform, and will test your resources fully. Although the opportunities in a game will be few, you should increase the chances of being completely successful when the moment arises by having spent time practising with a goalkeeper. Unfortunately, it is impossible to generalise as to the best moment for the individual run, there are far too many factors to be taken into consideration, but with increasing experience, *your* choice of moment and *the best* moment will coincide. When it happens you will know at once, and at the same time you will realise the difficulty of teaching that moment to somebody else.

Finally a forward should be enterprising and full of ideas to outwit the opposition. She should take the initiative positively and execute all her moves confidently and since confidence will not develop without skill we return to the subject of PRACTICE.

POSITIONAL PLAY

Wings

Thoroughly familiarise yourself with your position and understand the importance of good positioning. First consider the line up: train yourself to stand right on the side line, some players even start outside the field of play. This is to ensure that the space in which the forward line can operate is as large as possible. Left wings can often be seen dribbling the ball along the line with their feet off the field—remember, a ball is only off the field when it is wholly over the line. I agree that this is carrying space awareness to extremes, but the message is clear, the more space you can leave or create, the happier your team will be with you.

In Defence—When your defence are under pressure, all forwards should be prepared to assist, not by rushing into the mêlée but by carefully positioning themselves on the end of a clear channel, so enabling the defence to clear directly to them. Very often this escape route will find you deep in defence and sometimes so square that you will be on a line with the front edge of the circle and in the tramlines of course. Positioning for free hits or hit outs may be much the same, however, in your efforts to relieve the pressure by going deep into the defensive area your opposing team may get wise to your move, so have an understanding with your defence, that, if the clear channel develops forward you will be prepared to change your position and sprint hard for the forward pass ahead into the space. Incidentally, this is by far the quicker and more destructive method of cutting deep into the opposition's defence.

Should you win a roll in the defending area have a very close understanding with your half-back so that she knows what sort of roll you are wanting. In defence, it is better to try and gain as much ground as possible and quickly; therefore, position yourself behind the side line (feet and stick) and practise getting off the mark quickly to a ball rolled hard down the sideline, or as near to it as possible, gathering it on your stick. The closer the ball is to the side line and the harder it is rolled, the more chance you have of beating your opposing half-back. If she should challenge for the ball, anticipate the stick, dodge and concentrate on accelerating past her; then, according to the positioning of the opposing defence and your own forward line, make your decision as to the next move. Should your opponent be particularly fast, aim to rid yourself of the ball early whilst you are clear; since her turn and sprint will be fractionally behind yours, you will have time.

In Attack—Many wings have the idea that their job is to take the ball up the wing and then to centre in the circle area; these wings will not get far on the ladder of success—with only one tactic in mind their play will be very monotonous and easy to anticipate. Her real aim is to provide opportunities for her team to score, if not herself, and the more tactics she employs to keep the opponents guessing the better. Certainly, there are occasions when a wing will take the ball up the field and centre hard, but the point to bear in mind is whether she will arrive in the attacking 25 with an incomplete defence ahead. If so, look for the clear channel to the unmarked forward and centre hard and accurately; but if the dribble up-field results in none of the defence having been beaten, the spaces will be hard to find and the centre will probably be intercepted by the opposition. An early centre—somewhere after the defending 25—is often an intelligent move and if executed rapidly and accurately will provide an excellent opportunity for a dangerous attack. In this instance, it is often the centre-forward or distant inner who is free to receive your centre, and do be ready if you are included again in the flowing and rapid attacking move.

Do take the time carefully to watch the opposition's defensive covering, and, having understood it, make use of your knowledge in the choice of passes you make. If you should arrive at the circle edge in possession of the ball and with the complete defence ahead you may have three possible choices.

(1) Dribble your way through the opposition and shoot from an acute angle (recommended as a variation for the expert).

(2) Try to find the gap to centre across in front of and just out of reach of the goalkeeper for a rushing forward to deflect into goal.

(3) Pass slightly backwards to the forwards waiting on the circle edge on the other side of the field.

Should you arrive at the back line in possession:

(1) Again jinx and swerve to rid yourself of the opposition before shooting.

(2) Try a pass back either to your own wing-half or centre-half. Be careful you do not become a menace by being offside, either retreat rapidly or get off the field smartly (not recommended as a constructive method of escape).

With so little choice, you will realise how emphatic I am that a wing should base her game, together with the rest of the forwards, on arriving at the circle edge with as few defence in position as possible—the tactics chosen in this venture will depend on both the position of the ball and the position of the opposition.

Do not allow your presence to be forgotten. This can happen, particularly in circle play. If a team in attack concentrates on its inside forwards, the wing halves tend to move in to the area of play leaving the wings as free as air. Do enlighten your team. Position yourself ready for the quick shot, i.e. close in to the edge of the circle and on a line with the rest of your forwards, gauge your angle with the goal and then be prepared. If the ball is on the opposite side, you will probably find that the defence marking will move away from you in favour of marking the inner, believing you to be too far away to be of any danger. However, a quick, well-directed pass, perhaps from a half-back, may well surprise the opposition and give you your opportunity to shoot.

Rolls in the attacking half of the field do vary in possibilities owing to the diminishing space ahead. The wing should be prepared to adapt her positioning to the situation of less space and be prepared to use her team with prompt and short passes. In the attacking 25 it is often a sensible move for the wing herself to take the roll (so do not forget to learn something of the art of rolling) (see page 76), the reason being that the half tends to be drawn badly out of position and the left-wing has a very confined space in which to move before being offside. Wings are

often penalised for offside so do remember that you cannot be
offside if, either you are behind the striker or roller at the moment
the ball is hit or rolled in, or there are at least three opponents
between you and the goal.

Essentials to Practise

(1) Dribble the ball at top speed and be particularly conscious
of the value of acceleration and deceleration and the swerve.

(2) Centre the ball hard and through the gaps in the defence.
There is nothing more infuriating than a wing making a brilliant
run, outstripping the rest of the field and presenting the ball
right to the stick of the opposition.

(3) Time centring the ball at the exact moment the space appears,
which means being able to centre the ball at top speed and off
either foot. (See Plate 13.) A wing who takes too long in preparing
to centre signals her intentions to the opposition.

(4) Do disguise the angle of the centre until the very last
moment.

(5) When waiting to receive a pass, indicate exactly where you
want the ball.

(6) Hard, accurate and flat corner hits taken from all the positions (see Chapter 5).

(7) An understanding with both the wing-half and the inner.
The most rewarding passes that you can receive are those made
into the space ahead of you for you to accelerate and make
ground, and invariably it is the half or the inner you have to
thank—so be sure that you are all working on the same 'wave-
length', otherwise many good passes will go astray.

(8) Wings and inners should be partners, so use each other in
the preparation of a forward pass. The preliminary square pass
is a great space opener if followed by a through or forward pass.
(See Triangular Pass, page 15.)

(9) Do consider the conditions in deciding the strength of your
centre—a hard 'wallop' is not always the best kind of centre.

(10) Shoot goals. The more aggressive you can be in the circle,
the more space you will create for your inside forwards as the
wing halves are obliged to mark you. Should they drift towards
the middle, you are free to shoot.

Left Wings

It is surprising that top-class wings seem to be in short supply these days. To play left wing well, the basic essentials on which to build your game are speed, and the ability to centre the ball hard.

The difficulty you have to contend with is getting your feet around the ball to centre accurately whilst running at top speed. The technique involves:

either

an increase in your speed to overtake the ball so that is positioned on your right and slightly behind you,

or

one less tap in your dribble so that the ball is left behind in the correct position ready to be hit.

The correct position of the ball and the centre must be achieved promptly, otherwise your intention becomes too obvious. Realise that the drive must be made off either foot—whichever is leading at the moment of opportunity—and try not to upset the natural running action though you will have to acquire 'swivel hips' for the hit. Perhaps I should explain that swivel hips is an expression describing the path of the feet travelling forward whilst the trunk is rotated to the right in order to make the drive. The extent of this twist will depend on the required angle of the centre. Some players find it easier to chassé step around the ball in order to centre; the snag here is that the preparation indicates to the opposing defence the intended path of the ball. Train yourself to twist quickly and take your swing straight back, bringing it swiftly down and maintaining a strong follow-through.

The reverse stick hit is a must for left wings, both as a surprise move to catch the defence off guard, and in saving a number of seemingly hopeless situations when the ball is almost off the back line. With a reverse stick pass aimed back toward the centre of the circle another forward can make better use of the ball. Once your inside forwards know of your ability with the reverse stick they would be very unintelligent if they allowed themselves to wait for the ball, marked by an opponent.

Most of the passes will come to you from the right, so do practise receiving a variety of balls—slow balls will need meeting and perhaps you will have to dodge if you have the opposition in close attendance. Fast balls to your stick will demand extra resilience in your wrists, and fast balls into the space will demand anticipation and acceleration. If at full stretch you feel the ball will pass you, try reversing your stick, holding it firmly in the left hand and with a sweeping movement keep the ball in play. As soon as possible, catch up in order to get both hands on to the stick, enabling you to be at full strength for any emergency. (For Reverse Stick Play, see page 21.)

Right Wings

Disregard any comments you may hear that right wing is the easiest position on the field. If you play it, you know that it has problems, viz:

there is less of a shooting angle,
the angle of the pass to the right wing has to be more accurate,
there is an apparent lack of space.

However, let us consider something not quite as difficult—most of your passing will be to the left—choosing the right moment to pass or centre should be your aim, bearing in mind the importance of accuracy because the ball coming across the field is on the interceptor's easy side. Try to find the space just behind the waiting defence (and do not forget that defenders can run backwards), and put the ball across at speed to your own forward line.

Which foot you 'hit off' should be immaterial—practise using both to such a degree that you can centre at will, but do remember to manoeuvre the ball to your left just before you hit in order to achieve a flat centre. The angle of the centre depends upon the positioning of the opposition—each situation is never the same as the last, therefore it is essential to look for the gap before you centre.

Right wings very often find themselves cutting in to meet the ball. Beware of staying in and confining the playing area; either deliberately work for the interchange or swerve back and try to draw the opposition out toward you—if you succeed you will spread the defence and create more space for the attack. One of the backs is a player worth tempting; for then you will be drawing her well out of position—but do be sure she does not rob you of the ball.

Encourage your inner into giving you the sort of passes you feel that you can use best. Also, be alive to her needs both in attack and defence and always make yourself free for at least a square pass—the amount of space ahead will depend upon the positioning of your opposing left half. However, after a good preparatory square pass there is nearly always space ahead for the triangular return, enabling you to make ground rapidly and centre. There are occasions when a 'go it alone' policy will pay dividends—either as a surprise measure to gain some respect from the opposition, or simply because you see an opportunity to get through to the goal.

Being so close to the side line you should consider how to create space for yourself—for instance, if you wish to right dodge your opponent, swerve to your left in the approach run in order that you draw her to your left, so creating more space on her non-stick side.

At rolls, do make every effort to *control the ball* on your stick. It really is quite infuriating to see wings letting the ball run to their opponents.

If you ever have trouble with spectators crowding you, do not be frightened to appeal to the umpire for help, it could be disastrous to trip over a foot. Spectators can be noisy too, but do not let them upset your concentration, particularly when play is on the farther side, keep your wits about you and never let a cross pass go abegging.

What more can anybody ask than that you shoot goals, put across calculated centres and help your defence under pressure?

Inside Forwards

These are often the schemers of a team, and though each has an individual style, there are many points common to all;

Firstly—an ability to move in a somewhat confined space is essential, particularly so for the Centre-Forward, who can be completely enclosed by the opposition. *Close control of the ball* is vital and should become automatic with practice; this coupled with a thinking brain, which can assess a situation and make the correct decision at least 90 per cent of the time, helps to make a dangerous inside-forward. For this spontaneous assessment, an appreciation of each other's position is a necessity—in order to know of their problems and opportunities.

As inside-forwards you are so involved in the game that you can almost dictate the way in which it is played. The onus of distribution to the right person at the right time is upon your shoulders.

Watch the opposing defence for signs of weakness. It may be:

(1) that the Goalkeeper has difficulty in clearing with her left foot,

(2) the Right Back finds it difficult to tackle the left dodge,

(3) the Left Back is slow and is not able to cover sufficiently quickly following a cross pass

(4) the Centre-Half is often tempted to tackle the inners—leaving a free Centre-Forward

(5) the Left Half comes a long way in, leaving a forward space to the Wing,

(6) that, in circle, the Right Half does not mark on the goal stick and ball side of her opponent, leaving the left Inner free for a quick pass and shot.

etc. etc.

A team is as strong as its weakest link, for which you must learn to look and spot for yourselves and then put your exploiting tactics into operation.

When you have not got the ball, concentrate on good positioning, i.e. assess the situation and anticipate where you may best be used in attack. Even though your team may be deep in defence, make yourself free on a free escape route, but do indicate clearly where you want the ball.

Having received the ball, your object is to pass the defence, but beware of possible pitfalls:

(1) Hanging on to the ball and doing too much when there are players better positioned than you are to press the attack.

(2) Starving your wings of passes—this will result in the opposing wing halves closing in on the inside forwards, making even less room for you to move.

(3) Signalling your intentions by either:

    (a) taking too long to manoeuvre

    (b) looking up at the person to whom you are about to make the pass.

Now this does not mean that you do not look at all, that would be foolish—but it is intended to draw your attention to the good forward—who either glances around or has already assessed the situation before receiving the ball and dribbles in such a way that she notices any changes.

(4) Beware of looking at the corner of the goal into which you intend shooting—the reasons are obvious.

ESSENTIALS TO PRACTISE:

(1) Well-executed dodges which must be practised against opposition for disguise and split-second timing.

(2) Accurate close passing to beat an opponent.

(3) Accuracy in shooting with a variety of shots.

(4) The deliberate drawing of an opponent out of position followed by a quick pass or shot.

(5) Acceleration and deceleration. Although many players can run fast only few realise the value in changing speed, ending with a quick burst as a method of beating an opponent. Denise Parry, one of the best forwards in the world today, is a great exponent of this art and if you get the opportunity to watch her play you too will see the value of a change of speed. A sudden deceleration can surprise the opposition into over-running itself.

(6) Corners are an opportunity to shoot at goal—do make the most of these opportunities.

(7) Swerving—a forward who can swerve with the ball under control can pose problems to a defence, particularly if she can combine it with a change of speed. (See Plate 11.)

(8) Cultivate a variety of shots at the goalkeeper and train yourself to notice her difficulties and preferences. Many people do not realise the importance of a particularly good first shot, for if you give the goalkeeper feeble ones she will soon get her eye in and gain confidence at your expense.

(9) Rushing the goalkeeper. (See page 45.)

Left Inner

This position is considered by some to be the most creative and rewarding position on the field. Certainly, some of the greatest forwards of the past have been left inners, such as Marjorie Pollard, Mary Russell-Vick, Vera Chapman—these players have revelled in the ability to produce first-class stick work and ball control, a mass of original ideas and the expert's skill of execution.

Let us consider goals first—your prime object. Your team will expect you to be among the goal scorers and you will fail them if you are not. The majority of passes will be coming from your right to the stick side of your body—therefore, you have an obvious and immediate advantage in shooting. Practise shooting: from close in, from the edge of the circle, from tight angles near the back line with a variety of shots, i.e. flick, push, drive, reverse stick hit. With great accuracy look for the gaps the goalkeeper may leave just inside the nearside post. Also view the far post, which is her non-stick side. Many goals can be scored from close quarters by an unselfish left inner who, having dodged her way into the circle and drawn the goalkeeper toward her, uses a free right inner or right wing on the other side of the circle with a quick push pass—which, we hope, is unhesitatingly turned into the goal. (Fig. 28).

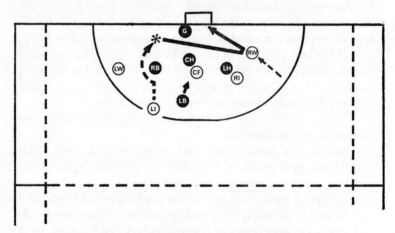

Fig. 28. The pass across the goalmouth

A similar situation can occur on finding yourself too close to the back line to be of any real use. Using the reverse stick, pass across the goal circle into a space in front of goal.

In mid-field keep the game open by using the wings—the right wing will be more difficult to find, but do not be deterred, bring her into the game with a really well-directed cross pass. If you take the trouble to understand the defensive covering, you will know that, following a cross pass, the covering is expected to move into the attack with the right back moving back to cover—so that in taking the initiative and crossing the ball you have forced the defence to move, in order to cope with your attack.

Partnership with the left wing is vital. Know the sort of passes each of you prefers and use each other to get round the opposing right half and in turn the right back. This means that you should be on hand for the square pass and if you are quick with your controlling of the pass, return a forward pass, aiming roughly for the corner flag. Your left wing should then have a satisfying sprint for the ball so long as you hit it at the correct speed. The left wing can be very useful to you in attack, particularly when the ball has been on the other side of the field. In the standard covering system the defence usually leave the wing who is farther from the ball in favour of marking another player closer to the goal. In this situation, keep your left wing in mind for a quick square pass from which she may be able to shoot. Incidentally, you will be a much sought after left inner if you give your left wing plenty of opportunities to shoot goals.

In trying to dislodge a well-positioned right half, you can sometimes tempt her to drop her guard of the forward space by dribbling toward her. Then you can put a through pass up the tramlines on her non-stick side to your wing, who should have anticipated your intention and gained a few yards start. This may lead to an interchange; but whatever transpires, you must make up your lost ground as fast as you can so that you too are on the shooting line in the circle.

Be 'in the know' at rolls and position yourself relative to the left wing and left half, making the best possible use of the space. On the whole, you will probably find yourself using the left dodge more often than the other dodges, simply because you are keeping the ball with you. If you part company with it, as in the right dodge, from your positioning on the field you are in danger of losing the ball to opponents in the centre of the field, so practise your left dodge until you could almost do it blindfold.

At corners, it is most useful, when the opposing defence is running out at top speed to spoil your shot (and what pleasure it is), to sidestep and feel her rush by, leaving you time and space to make a really good shot. In mentioning shots at a corner, cultivate a strong flick from the edge of the circle; you are in a very convenient position when receiving the ball from the left, to get some real force behind the shot and follow up quickly.

Centre-Forward

You could never feel lonely as a centre-forward—there are far too many people concerned with your whereabouts!

If you have always played centre-forward right from the first years, there will come a moment when your game should undergo a radical change. In the early years you may have been attracted to the position for various reasons; perhaps you knew the names of the players who start the game with a bully or perhaps you wanted to be in the 'thick of things'. Whatever your reasons for starting, they will not be the same for continuing.

A good centre-forward is a knowledgeable player particularly concerning positioning when she has not got the ball. In fact, some of the most interesting games are made by a centre-forward who hardly touches the ball at all but just enough to arrive free in the circle at the right spot to make contact and shoot.

To explain: the centre-forward is considered to have more opportunities to shoot than any other forward, so the centre-half, in an orthodox defensive system, is detailed to mark her closely (and no one else) and yet to intercept passes and distribute the ball to her own forwards. This task is made extremely difficult if the centre-forward can draw her out of position in order that the passes may go across the field unobstructed. This manoeuvring is accomplished by the centre-forward's anticipation of her team's moves and distracting the centre-half's attention by darting into new positions long enough for the ball to cross the field. I join some footballers in calling it 'moving off the ball'. If you like, it is 'leading the centre-half up the garden path' or 'selling a dummy'.

As the area is so confined, the centre-forward has to be an artist at creating space; the knack is to move away from the person with the ball. As the centre-half will be anxious to keep an eye on you she too will be drawn away, and at this point a watchful and cunning centre-forward will time her 'cut' (dash for the ball) to arrive round on the ball side of the centre-half at the same moment the ball arrives.

Another way of seemingly creating space is to be extremely sparing with the area in which you manoeuvre. The neater your dodges and the quicker your execution of a variety of shots, the better. The value of sudden darts and surprise stops will all help to outwit your opposition, and if you do find yourself out of position, inter-change confidently, revel in the freedom, and if the centre-half comes with you, be ready to make use of the space you have both left behind. If you have an understanding with your forwards to switch positions, somebody will be only too anxious to step into your space.

Right Inner

Although the inside-forwards have much in common, each position is distinctive, and none more so than the Right Inner.

As Right Inner, many of your passes will arrive from players on the left. In concentrating on meeting and controlling the ball, beware of two tendencies:

(a) to wait for the ball to come to you
(b) to waste time in allowing the ball to cross your body before controlling it.

In both instances, the time factor is of prime importance. Go to meet the ball, even if the pass is so slow it draws you right out of position; an interchange, a swerving run or a reverse stick dodge will soon get you on the goalward run.

Often the passes will come to you square, in which case you may be nearly or actually stationary; this need not be a bad thing if you can sprint suddenly and use the change of speed to surprise and outwit your 'shadows'.

Your right wing will rely on you to bring her into the game, and indeed you must, but notice the opposing left half, her stick side will normally cover your long forward pass unless she is out of position, either being drawn so or perhaps being left behind. In tempting her to cover her non-stick side, react swiftly with the forward pass the moment you see the angle opening. As with the left wing, the right wing will 'bless' you as she streaks for the long ball. At this point, do not dilly dally, marvelling at your prowess, but quickly get back on the shooting line; you will have quite a distance to make up.

The right dodge will probably be your most useful individual method of beating an opponent, because although you momentarily lose contact with the ball, it is made into the space and remember, the smaller the push forward the quicker you will regain the ball. Incidentally, I have no patience with players who deliberately make a right dodge, putting the ball toward a player of the opposite side and then looking hurt when the Umpire refuses to award a free hit for obstruction as the third player runs off with the ball!

Glorious passes do come across from the left aimed diagonally forward for the right wing. With a swift acceleration and left-hand lunge at full stretch, you gather the ball at top speed. Then, find the gap down the centre, caused by the two backs changing from covering to attack, and once through or round the covering back, you have only the goalkeeper to beat.

Again, I stress the importance of watching the defensive system for loopholes—herein lies the opportunity to scheme your attack.

The non-stick side of the centre-half is a target to exploit. Angle your pass but not too near the covering back; you must serve the centre-forward so that she can have controlled the ball before being faced with the opposition.

A good cross pass to either the left wing or left inner is essential. (Refer to cross passing on page 86.)

4 Goalkeeping

Goalkeeping is both exciting and challenging; a position requiring quick reactions, determination and a resilient sense of humour to rise above dismaying situations which sometimes occur. Anywhere else on the field a mistake can be quickly rectified—for the goal-keeper there is seldom a second chance. A motto to be metaphoric-ally nailed to the goalpost is that which President Truman had on his desk—'The buck stops here!'

A good goalkeeper makes the job look easy, the ball always seems to come straight to her because from experience of studying the opposing forwards she knows their favourite dodges and can be, literally, one jump ahead. A forward approaching the goal with the ball has the odds on her side, at that moment she has the chance of scoring. The fun of goalkeeping is that by intelligent positioning and anticipation you can transfer the odds to your favour, stop the ball and quickly put your own team on the attack.

KICKS

The basic kick is a sweeping one using the inside of the foot round about the big-toe joint. It is used for clearing the ball to the sides—safely sweeping it away from oncoming forwards—and always for first-time clearances where the power of the shot can be used to augment the kick.

The toe kick is best for stationary or slow-moving balls; remem-ber the area of contact is smaller than with the side kick therefore the margin of error is greater.

Whatever type of kick is used it is essential to bend the knees as you move into it, keep the weight well forward on the toes and your head over the ball, watching it intently. The foot which is not doing the kicking must be close beside the ball at the moment of impact; this will ensure the clearance is flat and powerful. In any ball game the difference between the mediocre player and the star is the extent to which the ball is watched. Watch it all the way to your foot—do not *imagine* you are watching it—make *sure* you are. There is a subtle difference.

A simple check on balance is to take another step forward after a kick—if you can still move ahead your weight is right, if not the weight must be on your heels.

POSITIONING (See Plates 1, 2 and 3)

A goalkeeper is by no means stationary during a game; she must be aware of her exact position with relation to the goal at any

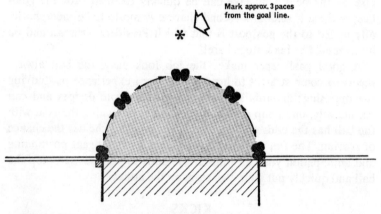

Mark approx. 3 paces
from the goal line.

Fig. 29. During the game, the G.K. positions herself on an imaginary goal semi-circle constantly moving in line with the ball

moment. Often there is no time to turn and check up on the goal-post, therefore before the game starts take two large paces out from the centre of the goal line and make a small mark in front of you, this will help keep track of your position whilst following the game, moving in a semi-circle from the goal posts (See Fig. 29). Do not carve a deep gash in the turf—just a scratch on the surface or some indentations tapped with the toe of the stick will do. Better still, you may be able to pick up a bit of white from the line to make a spot.

Some goalkeepers mark lines out from the goal posts as well, these are helpful but are difficult to mark on some dry surfaces, therefore it is wise not to become too reliant on them.

TACTICS

'What should I stop and what should I clear first time?' There are so many variables that it is impossible to give a categorical answer to this question; only experience will tell, but as a generalisation stop the hard one from the centre, it is difficult to kick this accurately into a safe area first time. Bend your knees as you stop the shot, this will trap the ball safely in front of you ready for a quick clearance—a rebound out of your reach can quickly become a goal; forwards do not need that much encouragement. With the ball at your feet and the forwards almost on you, clear to the left

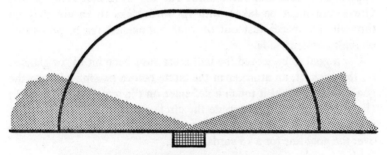

Shaded portion shows safest area for clearances.

Fig. 30. Clearances

with your stick (one-handed if necessary), keeping your feet firmly together behind the ball. If the forwards are not too close you will be able to kick the ball clear.

The shots that come in at an angle can be swept away with the inside foot kick. Keep your eye on the ball, the simplest-looking shot is often the hardest to deal with—watch those slow ones—they can spin and fool you.

The safest areas which to send the ball are to the sides; if an opponent does manage to collect the clearance she is in a position where a shot at goal can most easily be blocked (Fig. 30). A beginner should play for safety and use these areas all the time; firstly just to get the ball as far out as she can and later to direct it to one of her own team who should be prepared to receive it.

Be very careful not to give away corners, clearances too close to the back line are prone to spin over; learn to judge these accurately. Try to save deflections from your own players which would otherwise go over the back line for a corner; though it is not very sensible to rush out wildly in an attempt to save every single one, you may be leaving an open goal and an unmarked forward—be discriminating.

As you gain more confidence and accuracy you can take suitable opportunities to direct clearances in other spaces with a view to putting your team on the attack as quickly as possible. If your team has been defending, the opposing forwards and halves will be well up in the circle; an accurate clearance through these to your own forwards will put them away up the field in no time, leaving their opponents to turn and chase back. The key word here is ACCURACY. Great care must be taken with forward kicks to ensure they go through the spaces just out of your opponents' reach, preferably on their non-stick side.

For a goal to be scored the ball must have been hit by, or glanced off the stick of, an attacker in the circle before passing between the goal posts. (Should it touch a defender on the way it is still a goal.) If a shot is made from outside the circle and you are sure no other attacker will be able to rush in and touch it on the way, let it go over the goal line for a 15 yards hit out.

TEAMWORK

The secret of good goalkeeping is to THINK POSITIVELY. Think yourself part of your team's attack and you will be on your toes, rarin' to go, leaning forward absolutely ready for a quick move in any direction. If you think defensively and negatively you will be lolling back on your heels, in no position to deal rapidly with anything.

You must have a good understanding with your backs, they should allow you a clear sight of the ball at all times. Call out if they stand in the way; with co-operation you will find this occurs very little. Perhaps you will be able to help them by suggesting that if they can see you easily over their shoulder (without turning right round) you are most likely to have a good sight of the ball.

Discourage your defence from jabbing wildly at goal shots, they may well deflect them past you into the goal—and there is nothing more frustrating than having a goal scored against you by your own team.

Whenever possible the backs must tackle just outside the circle; move forward when this happens so that, should the back fail to win, you can get the ball before the attacker is able to control it for a shot. In a situation where there is no other defence player around, try to meet a breakaway forward as near the circle edge as possible, and make sure that your feet are together if the shot is made before you reach the forward; it is very frustrating to find the ball has gone between your feet as you ran.

In all cases the goalkeeper can completely block the shot if she can get right up to the attacker's stick.

Figs. 31A and 31B show how much of the goal line can be guarded in different positions. In each diagram the goalkeeper is drawn as 18 inches wide and coming out from the dead centre of the goal line. In Fig. 31A she has only to move 9 inches either side and the goal is covered—assuming she has anticipated correctly the side the forward is shooting.

In Fig. 31B she has to move four feet six inches each side, but she has more time as the ball has 13 yards to travel. Now for an interesting point: look at that side shot from the wing—how do they ever score? Actually it is quite simple—the goalkeeper does not stay tight against the post; believing that the goal is safely blocked she is tempted to move in slightly and the ball goes between her pads and the goalpost.

Concentrate *all* the time. Watch the opposing forwards; get to know their favourite dodge and passes, analyse their game and the odds will be on your side when you meet in the circle. A great many forwards would be horrified to realise how predictable they are.

PRACTICES

A great deal of practice beneficial to goalkeeping can be carried out away from the hockey pitch. Any games which improve footwork and agility such as squash or basketball are a great help.

Make use of any small space you have available; use a tennis ball or a light plastic ball of any size and kick it against a wall—preferably one with an irregular surface or a corner which will give a variable return. Try throwing the ball at the wall with your eyes shut, opening them in time to block the return.

Ask a friend to throw some balls at you to practise hand stops. High shots at goal may be saved with the hand but the ball may not be propelled in any direction, you must drop it immediately to

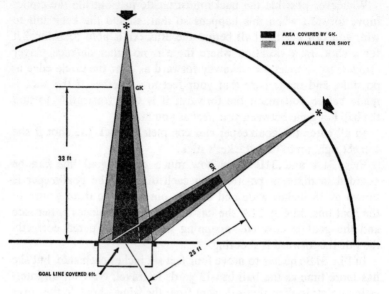

AREA COVERED BY GK.
AREA AVAILABLE FOR SHOT

GK

33 ft

GK

25 ft

GOAL LINE COVERED 6ft.

Fig. 31A. Narrowing the shooting angle

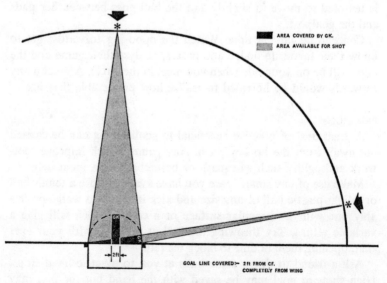

AREA COVERED BY GK.
AREA AVAILABLE FOR SHOT

GK

2ft

GOAL LINE COVERED:~ 2ft FROM CF.
COMPLETELY FROM WING

Fig. 31B. Guarding the goal line

the ground. You will be penalised if you take part in the game without a stick in your hand, so be careful not to drop it in your efforts to stop the ball with your hand.

Wearing pads and kickers, dribble a hockey ball in and out of a line of obstacles (skittles, etc.). Check yourself against a stop watch to provide a speed challenge, it is not very difficult just doodling along slowly but increase the speed and your ball control will have to be much better.

On a hockey pitch place two sets of skittles as shown in Fig. 32 and a few hockey balls round the edge of the circle. As a forward

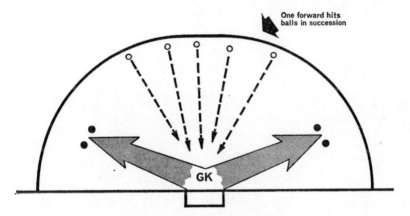

Fig. 32. Skittle practice for G.K.

hits the ball at you in succession, clear them to whichever side is appropriate to the shot. Adjust the spacing between the skittles and the speed of the shots as you become more skilful.

Two goalkeepers can practise kicking a ball to each other between skittles; make sure that both feet are used. A goalkeeper must be 'ambidextrous'—or should it be 'ambipedrous'?

General team practices should be organised so that they end with a shot at goal and thus keep the goalkeeper working as part of a team rather than feeling a solitary soul who must practise away in a corner until she is called in to be the Aunt Sally for endless shooting practice. Subtlety of approach is required in practices, not a cannonade of shots which can only end in unnecessary bruising.

Goalkeeping requires initiative and both in play and in practice you must sort out the problems yourself. This chapter is intended as a general guide, and, hopefully, a spur to great achievement. You will make mistakes, everyone does, but as long as you learn something from them, you will improve rapidly.

Turn to page 159 for details of equipment.

5 Set Play

CORNERS

A *long corner* is given when the ball is sent unintentionally over the back line by a member of the defence. It is hit from a point five yards from the corner of the field. Most wings take corners from the point five yards along the back line as it is easier for the forwards to receive the ball from that angle—however, on particularly bumpy grounds, it is sometimes good policy, particularly on the left, for the attack to hit the corner from a point five yards up the side line. From this angle, though slightly more difficult to receive, more forwards are positioned in the circle ready to shoot should the first player miss the ball. Long corners should be particularly efficient if they are to be effective. The ball has to travel farther from the 'hitter', which means that the defence have longer time to run out from behind the back line to mark their opponents.

A *short corner* or penalty corner is given for an infringement in the circle by a member of the defence, or if one of them deliberately clears the ball over the back line. Also in the case of a deliberate foul by a member of the defence anywhere in the defending 25 yards area. It can be taken from either side of the goal at a point on the back line ten yards from either goal post.

ATTACKING CORNERS (See Plate 10)

The player taking the corner should hit the ball hard, flat and accurately:

(1) Hard, because it gives less time for the defence to get out to spoil the shot
(2) Flat, because it is easier to stop
(3) Accurately, because it takes less time to control.

A 'pushed' corner is a useful variation as its intended destination can be disguised until the last moment. Do not forget to get back 'onside' before rejoining the forward line. Corner hitting is an art which few players seem prepared to practise—place the ball, taking care to avoid any bumps or depressions—position yourself sensibly (you may stand on the pitch) and at the same time notice the exact whereabouts of your waiting forwards. Keep your head over the ball and concentrate on hitting the ball firmly, aiming for the exact spot where the waiting forward wants it. The back lift and follow-through play an important part in attaining accuracy—any deviation off a straight swing will cause the ball to do something peculiar. Practise hitting a target 20 yards distant.

WAITING FORWARDS

Keep well spaced, though edge a little toward the corner hitter, more so for the long corner than the penalty corner. If you are consistent in where you position yourself, it should help your accuracy. For example, if the centre-forward stands opposite the left-hand post for corners taken on the left, and opposite the right-hand post for corners on the right, she gives herself an immediate shooting angle without wasting time to look up and take aim. To practise:

(1) Stopping the ball on the exact spot you want it. This is quite an art and requires much practice. If the ball 'pops' away from your stick, you are wasting your time and giving more chance to the defence to spoil the shot.

(2) Accuracy; the obvious places to aim for are just inside each goal post, so if your starting position is reasonably consistent, you can practise your shooting angle to a very high degree of proficiency. Place a target just inside each post.

(3) Speedy execution of the whole movement of hitting hard, receiving and shooting. The quicker you can make your shot, the less distance the oncoming defence will have covered. As you wait for the corner note the exact position of the posts, line up your shooting angle, and stand in such a way as to be ready both to stop and hit with the minimum amount of movement. Stop the ball in the most convenient spot for making the shot and then shoot quickly—the shorter the back lift the better.

(4) 'The follow up'; do not wait to see whether the goalkeeper saves, but follow up the shot as soon as possible. If you arrange

to receive the corner in a certain order, it helps the 'non-receivers' to 'rush' at the very first opportunity.

Having attained a good standard in the basic technique, let us turn to tactics. The surprise element gives a fraction more time,

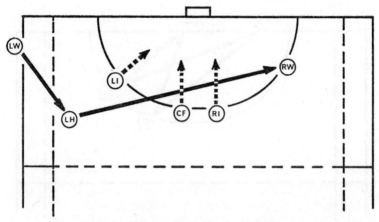

Fig. 33. Forward tactics—Variation 1

so consider some of the following tactics, remembering that the weaker side of the orthodox defensive covering system is farther from the ball.

Variation 1 (Fig. 33). The left wing takes the corner from 5 yards up the side line—hits the ball to the left half, meanwhile the

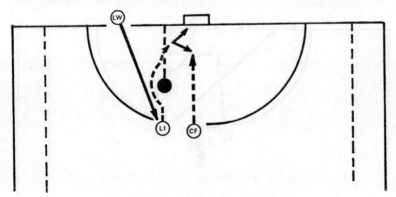

Fig. 34. Forward tactics—Variation 2

waiting forwards move toward the goal, creating the space behind them so that the left half can hit the ball really hard across to the free right wing.

Variation 2 (Fig. 34). This corner is hit to the left inner who moves toward the back line dodging an opponent to shoot, or, depending

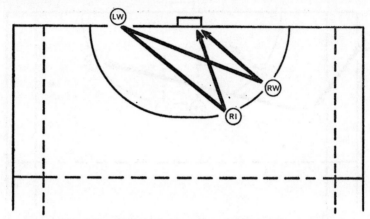

Fig. 35. Forward tactics—Variation 3

on the spaces, passes across the goal mouth for the centre-forward or right inner to shoot.

Variation 3 (Fig. 35). The left wing must have a really hard drive in order to get the ball to the right inner or right wing in time to use it effectively.

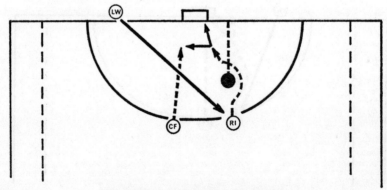

Fig. 36. Forward tactics—Variation 4

Variation 4 (Fig. 36). The ball is hit to the right inner who moves toward the oncoming right half, dodges her, and shoots at close range. Sometimes, instead of shooting, there is an opportunity to make a square pass to her left for the centre-forward or left inner to shoot.

Variation 5 (Fig. 37). The centre-forward lessens the time factor by handstopping for the poised left inner to shoot at the corner of the goal. It is essential to arrange 'the hitter' to the left of the 'hand-stopper', and to receive the ball coming from the left as otherwise

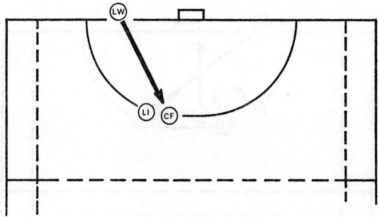

Fig. 37. Forward tactics—Variation 5

the bodies get in each other's way. This variation demands a high degree of proficiency. The 'handstopper' must remember to stop the ball absolutely stationary otherwise the umpire will penalise her for moving the ball illegally. Try to stop the ball with the hand *behind* the ball, not on top.

Variation 6 (Fig. 38). Whilst the corner is being hit to the right inner, the centre-forward foils the opposing centre-half by running towards the goal—thus creating space for the waiting centre-half to step into the circle to shoot.

N.B. There is nothing in the rules stating who should take or receive corners, so although I have indicated the more normal positions, there is no reason why other players should not step in to 'throw' the opposition. For instance, if you have a particularly hard-hitting left back, give her an opportunity to shoot, or, if you have a 'flat' accurate hitter, ask her to take the corner and bring in the wing to shoot.

Beware:

(1) Offside. Every player involved in corners must be alive to the position of the third member of the defence, and if she is missing, keep behind the player who has the ball.

(2) Corner tactics are fun to work out—but do not sacrifice the good direct method of attack for more complicated schemes poorly executed.

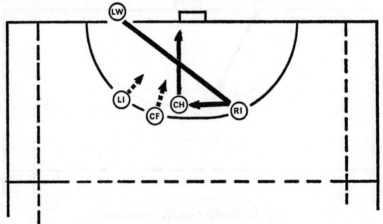

Fig. 38. Forward tactics—Variation 6

DEFENDING CORNERS

Positioning behind the back line, opposite their opponents' sticks.

Though showing the opposition sensibly placed around the edge of the circle (Fig. 39), I have not indicated their positional names, so that you are not surprised by a sudden change of positions.

In defending a corner, the prime objective is to clear the ball from your circle to your waiting forwards. Therefore:

(1) Familiarise yourselves with the orthodox covering plan.

(2) If the wing half nearer the corner happens to be a particularly fast player, the back may be wise to relinquish her duty to go out to the inner and move to cover the wing.

(3) Position yourselves behind the back line opposite the stick side of your opponent.

(4) Watch the stick of the corner hitter and time your running forward to coincide exactly with the moment her stick contacts the ball.

(5) Train yourself to get off the mark as quickly as possible. In an effort to reach your opponent before the ball does, some

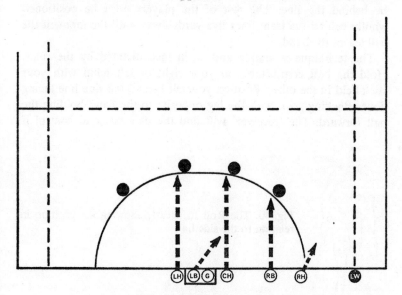

Fig. 39. Defending a corner

players move from a crouched position, others prefer a flying start; that is, start a few yards behind the back line, and as the hitter prepares, the defender starts to run, crossing the back line as the ball is hit.

(6) In running to challenge your opponent, keep your stick on the ground gripped firmly ready to tackle or intercept.

(7) In gathering the ball clear it accurately and as quickly as possible.

(8) Try to cope with surprise moves competently and without fuss. Once you show confusion, it will spur the forwards on.

THE ROLL IN

On the whole 'rolls' are a neglected part of the game. Having gained possession of the ball, it seems a waste not to plan to use it to the best advantage.

The rules stipulate that the ball must touch the ground within one yard of where it went off. The feet and stick of the 'roller' must be behind the line. The rest of the players must be positioned wholly behind the tram lines five yards away until the moment the ball leaves the hand.

The technique is simple and is, in fact, dictated by the rules. Hold the ball comfortably in your right or left hand with your stick held in the other. Position yourself behind the side line facing your attacking goal, with the leg opposite to the hand holding the ball forward. The 'receiver' will find the ball easier to control if

Fig. 40. The Roll In, clearly showing the position in relation to the side line

it is running smoothly along the ground; so, at the same time as you swing your arm forward, bend your knees, making sure that the back of the hand brushes the grass, to release the ball at ground level. Rolls that bump along the ground are usually the result of careless 'rollers' who forget to bend their knees (Fig. 40).

To be particularly effective, the ball is best rolled with the hand nearer to the side line—it not only helps to prevent poor positioning on or over the line, but makes the angle of the roll much easier to achieve. Practise accurate rolling by placing two posts some way away on the side line, then position yourself behind the side line and aim to roll the ball in between, using either hand.

Tactics: The wing half usually takes the 'roll in', but there is a good case for the wing taking it in the attacking 25-yard area. If

Plate 10. Penalty corner. (*England v. Scotland. Tunbridge Wells*). Notice: (1) The speed off the mark of the Scottish defence. (2) Both the English R.I. and C.F. are expecting the ball whilst the L.I. and L.W. prepare to move in to follow the shot. (3) The backing up of the English C.H. and L.H. (4) The Umpire has moved in to see play more clearly.

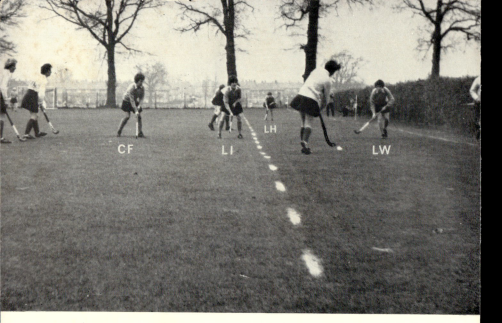

Plate 11. Ringing a free hit. (*Herts. v. Berks.*). The Berks. R.B. taking the free hit is faced with a ring of Herts. players—her escape route is via the R.W. who can be seen running back for a short pass.

Plate 12. A penalty bully. (*England v. Scotland*). Notice: (1) Positioning of the Umpire. (2) The rest of the players beyond the 25 yards line.

the half continues to take it, she is drawn completely out of position, whilst the wing's forward space is too cramped for much variety of ideas.

Successful rolls are essentially the result of good team work, therefore, carefully plan and practise your ideas. I put forward the following examples for a working basis, but do not forget the value of surprise:

(1) *The 'Long Roll'* (Fig. 41) is the most direct method of gaining ground and is particularly useful to move from the defend-

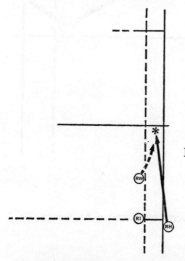

Fig. 41. The Long Roll

ing area and into the attack as quickly as possible. On the right side of the field, it is particularly effective to roll the ball as close to the side line as possible, as this is on the non-stick side of the opposing left half and, therefore, more difficult for her to intercept. The wing half should carefully note the positioning of the wing and opposing wing half and relate the speed of her roll to the distance between the two. (See Plate 9.)

(2) *Using the Surprise Element* (Fig. 42). The reverse roll is a particularly useful surprise move and often includes the back. Prepare to roll the ball forward but as the arm swings forward to a point level with the back foot, rotate the hand inwards and continue turning until releasing the ball at approximately right angles to the body.

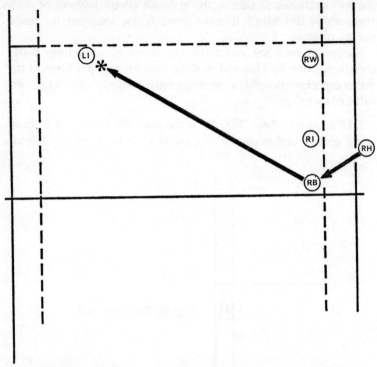

Fig. 42. Using the back with a reverse or short roll to change the direction of attack

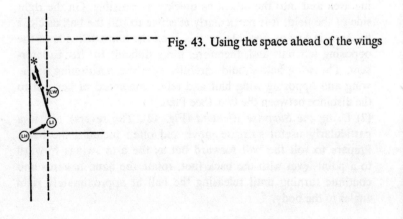

Fig. 43. Using the space ahead of the wings

(3) *Another method in using the space ahead of the wings* (Fig. 43). Here the left half uses the left inner who passes the ball at an angle forward into the space ahead of the left wing for her to run on to.

(4) *Another Variation* (Fig. 44). The left half rolls the ball to the left inner who returns it conveniently to the left half either

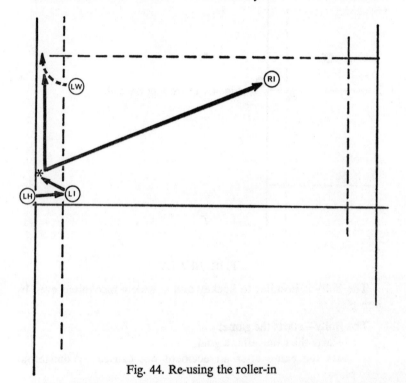

Fig. 44. Re-using the roller-in

to hit it up the side line to the left wing who has quickly moved out, or to make a cross pass to a free player on the other side of the field.

In selecting your rolls for use, consider

(1) Your whereabouts on the field and make the best use of the space available.

(2) The positioning of the opposition. There is no point in using complicated moves if the more simple and direct routes to a goal are free.

DEFENDING THE ROLL (Fig. 45)

In order to defend the roll effectively, the opposing wings and inners should assist by marking their opposing forwards—thus enabling the half and the back to mark the spaces.

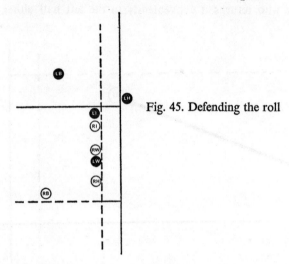

Fig. 45. Defending the roll

THE BULLY

The bully is peculiar to hockey and is widely recognised even by non-players.

The Bully—starts the game;
    re-starts the game after a goal;
    starts the game after an accident not caused by dangerous play;
    starts the game after a simultaneous breach of a rule by two opposing players;
    restarts the game following a penalty bully when the defence clears the ball out of the circle.

Technique

Keep your right hand well down your stick to ensure strength and control. To bully the ball, two players shall stand squarely facing each other and the side lines with their left shoulders pointing toward their attacking goal. They are required to 'strike first the ground on their side of the ball and then their opponent's stick over the ball three times alternately, after which one of the two players must strike the ball before it is in general play. The flat face of the stick only may be used for making contact with the opponent's stick in the bully. Every other player shall be nearer to her own goal line than the ball (except in the case of a penalty bully) and shall not stand within 5 yards of the players participating in the bully until the ball is in general play. A bully in the circle shall not be taken within 5 yards of the goal line'.

The idea is to gain possession of the ball and set up an attacking move as quickly as possible. Many people think that in order to win a bully, it must be quick—but this is not necessarily so. The most important part comes after the third tap of your opponent's stick—the player who gets her stick to the ball first will win possession. Let us suppose that your stick gets to the ball first—what next?—

(1) Pull the ball toward you out of your opponent's reach and either pass left or right or dribble away yourself.

(2) Push the ball away from you, aiming to pass to the right inner by way of the gap between your opponent's stick and right leg.

(3) Quickly reverse stick the ball back to the centre half or other player positioned likewise.

(4) If the sticks jam together momentarily, it is possible to 'pressure' the ball over the top of your opponent's stick in order to make use of it on the other side.

The position of the head is vital in winning bullies. In keeping your head over the ball, your weight must be forward over the toes, which means that you will be quicker off the mark. Do make up your mind which method you are going to attempt before starting, as it will make a difference to your footwork. For instance, if you intend pulling the ball toward you and passing to your left, you will have to adjust your left foot. On starting to bully, give your whole concentration to winning the ball.

PENALTY BULLY (See Plate 12)

The penalty bully is given when in the Umpire's opinion—

(a) A goal most probably would have been scored, but for a foul inside the circle by a member of the defending team, or

(b) There has been a wilful foul inside the circle, by a player of the defending team.

A penalty bully shall be played by the offender and by any player selected by the other team, on a spot 5 yards in front of the centre of the goal line. All other players shall be beyond the 25-yard line in the field of play, and shall not cross such 25-yard line, nor take any further part in the game until the penalty bully has been completed. When the goalkeeper is the guilty party, she loses the privilege of being able to kick the ball.

The defender is usually at a disadvantage, so I will start with her tactics. It is wise for her to keep calm, and not to rush the bully. Time the first two taps fairly slowly then come down quickly behind the ball after the third and try pushing it toward and past the forward. Keep on your toes so that you can follow up any advantage gained if your opponent moves backwards. Previous observation of bullies during the game may give you some indication of her favourite tricks.

From the attacker's point of view, you have everything to gain so try to keep the upper hand by dictating play as much as you can. Plan your method of beating the defender before you start; bully quickly in an effort to unsettle the defender further, and be very sure that, after the third tap, your stick gets to the ball first. After that the outcome is a test of skill.

The attacker wins a penalty goal, either:

(a) by scoring a goal,
(b) by virtue of a foul by the defender,
(c) by the ball being inadvertently deflected into the goal by the defender.

The defender stops a penalty goal either:

(a) by clearing the ball wholly out of the circle into the field of play,
(b) by the forward committing a breach of the rules,
(c) by the forward missing the goal and putting the ball off the back line.

The bully is retaken, if:

(a) it is not completed properly,
(b) the defender hits the ball over the goal line (but not between the posts),

(c) both players foul simultaneously,

(d) any other player interferes.

If a goal is not scored, play is restarted by a bully at the centre of the nearer 25-yard line. If necessary, extra time must be given for the completion of a penalty bully.

There is no secret formula for winning the bully—just practice. You may have a penalty bully only a few times in your whole playing career, but those moments may be very important to your team —so understand the rules and be prepared.

FREE HIT AND HIT OUT

A free hit is awarded to the opposing team when a player infringes one of the rules. No other player, apart from the 'hitter', may stand within 5 yards. It is taken on the spot where the breach occurred, except in the circle, where if the *attack* is awarded a free hit, it becomes a penalty corner, and if the defence is awarded a free hit it may be taken anywhere inside the circle. (The circle line is included within the boundaries of the circle.) Although most players take the hit from the circle edge, there is no reason why the ball should not be hit from ANYWHERE inside the circle. This is particularly useful for defence players to remember when you come to take a free hit, and find all your forwards or spaces marked by the opposition—change the angle of the escape route by quickly moving the ball to another part of the circle, and hitting it promptly to one of your own team.

As a general rule—free hits are most advantageous if they are designed to 'move' the opposing defence, either because the free hit is directed to a free player, and/or by switching the attack with a cross pass.

In or near the circle a free player standing in the circle or having space in the circle ahead of her should not be ignored. Within a well-drilled defence this is unlikely, but if the occasion does present itself—make the most of it.

The Hit Out

If the ball is sent out of play over the back line or the goal line and no goal is scored, by either a player of the attacking team or accidentally by a member of the defending team 25 yards or more distant from the back line, the game is restarted with a free hit to be taken by a player of the defending team exactly opposite the place where it crossed the back line, and 15 yards from the inner edge of that line.

To stand a chance of success, free hits and hit outs must be taken quickly and I cannot stress this point too emphatically, therefore the whole team should be alert, first in getting the ball to the appropriate spot, and secondly in making themselves free to be used. This obviously applies to forwards particularly, but there is no reason why members of the defence should not be equally accessible.

As to who should take free hits and hit outs—there is no rule. My advice, since speed is so important, is that the nearest defence player should consider it her responsibility and if this does cause her to be drawn slightly away from her area—the defence should be sufficiently flexible to cope.

Defending the free hit or hit out: If members of the team are the slightest bit slow in taking their hit, it is possible for the opposition to (i) mark the players, or (ii) ring the hitter. (See Plate 11.)

In mid-field—where space is at a premium—marking the players is probably the best system, although there is no hard-and-fast rule. Each forward marks the corresponding forward (and do not forget to be on both the ball and the stick side of that opponent); whilst the defence mark the spaces.

Near the circle, where space is more confined—ring the player with the ball.

As the opposition prepares to take the hit, the three or four nearest forwards should position 5 yards distant, whilst defence mark the gaps between. The 'hitter's' frustration and your quick eye to intercept the ball will often result in regaining possession of the ball. However be warned! One loose link and the tactic breaks down. Turn to Plate 11 facing page 77 and you will see the 'ring' in action.

Beating the 'Ring'. Once the 'ring' is in position this is a difficult task. However, there is a useful escape route via another free player standing at a little distance which is often parallel to the hitter. The hit must be taken quickly and the intention disguised until the very last moment. With the change of angle it should be possible to find a space to a forward.

In the following diagram (Fig. 46), this is shown at a 'hit out'.

Beating the player-to-player marking system. Again this is diffi-

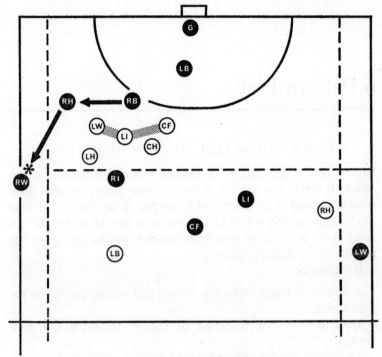

Fig. 46. Beating the 'Ring'

cult when all the opposition have had time to gain their marking positions—however, try to create space by moving away from the ball; your opponent will probably come with you, so that another member of the team may have the use of the space created by your moving.

6 Pattern Play

ATTACK IS THE BEST METHOD OF DEFENCE

Pattern play is designed for its efficiency in changing defence into attack. It makes the best use of the available space and relies upon accuracy, speed of execution and teamwork. A fast player dribbling the ball up the field will not cover the same amount of ground in a given time as precision passing movement, particularly when the players are strategically placed.

It requires:

Accuracy combining direction finding and sending the ball at the right speed.

Speed of execution including an efficient technique and good timing.

Teamwork involves an understanding as a result of discussion and practice of the various combinations and their consequences. (It could be calamitous to surprise your own team as well as the opposition.)

THE CROSS PASS (Figs. 47, 48, 49)

The cross pass is vital to a team intent on drawing the defence out of position, as it causes the whole defence to switch its covering.

It may be more difficult to get your feet round the ball to cross pass to the right, but the angle is very much easier to find than right to left, as the ball is crossing much of the centre-half's territory to her non-stick side. However, both directions are necessary for a balanced team, and every member of the team should look for the opportunity to switch the attack, making the pass hard and accurate—the quicker you do it the less chance the opposition will have to anticipate and intercept.

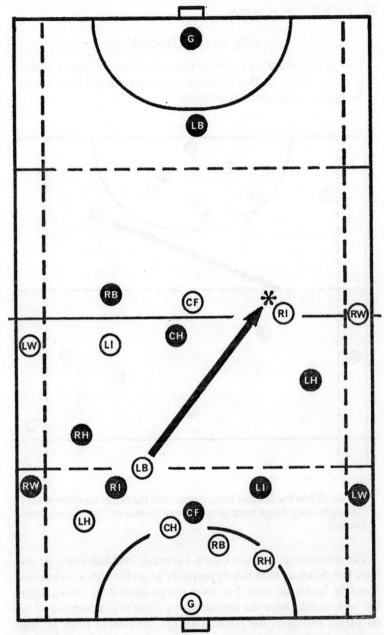

Fig. 47. Cross passing from the defence, effectively using the mid-field space

THE INTERCHANGE

This is a method of catching the opposition off guard, even if only momentarily, so that an attacking movement can be developed or brought to a successful conclusion.

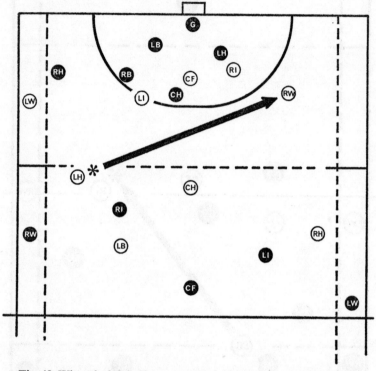

Fig. 48. When the left half cross passes near the circle, notice how the free right wing drops back to create more space in which to control the ball

The interchange can work both *Forwards and Sideways*. At present, few defences take this opportunity to go through with the ball. Shooting backs are rare, but when the moment does present itself, the back should have the confidence to know that a member of her own team will cover her position for her. Half-backs often get their opportunity to move into the attacking circle in possession of the ball, but almost always pass beforehand, perhaps believing that it

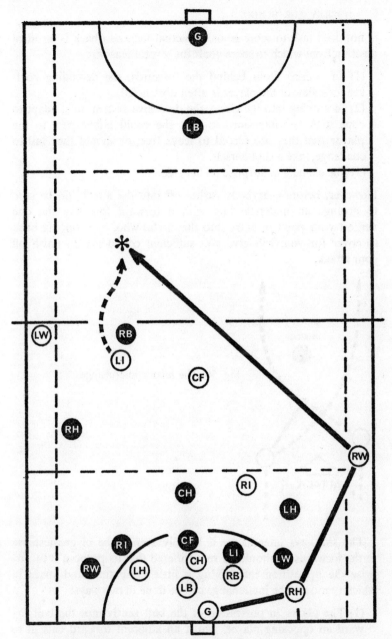

Fig. 49. Counter-attacking with an early cross pass can be devastating, particularly if more than one forward is up with the attack

is not their task to score goals. In actual fact, half-back is an ideal position from which to score goals for several reasons:

(1) In coming from behind the forwards, the defending goal-keeper's view of the player is often obstructed.

(2) In moving into the circle, the defensive system must adapt to cope with her intrusion, so that she could either pass to the player that they are forced to leave free, or should they fail to challenge, take a shot herself.

(3) The element of surprise on her side.

However, before everybody rushes off into the attack, do be sure to arrange an understanding with a forward (possibly the one nearest your point of entry into the circle) who, by dropping back to cover for you, will give you sufficient confidence to finish off your attack.

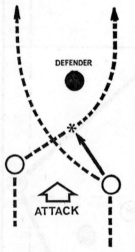

Fig. 50. The scissor interchange

The sideways interchange is usually seen to be of greatest use to the forwards. It should be remembered that its purpose is to surprise the opposition into giving a little more time and space in which to move. The interchange can be done in two ways:

(1) The player in possession of the ball gently taps the ball toward an opposing player, whilst an adjacent forward cuts in to meet it to change places with the 'tapper', hopefully leaving the opposition caught between the two (Fig. 50). It is important to

carry out this manoeuvre with either a rapid acceleration, or at top speed, and not to get within tackling range of the opposition. It is possible to vary this idea by cutting in and *dribbling* toward the opposition and at the last moment *pass* the ball square to an adjacent forward who has completed the scissor-like movement to exchange places.

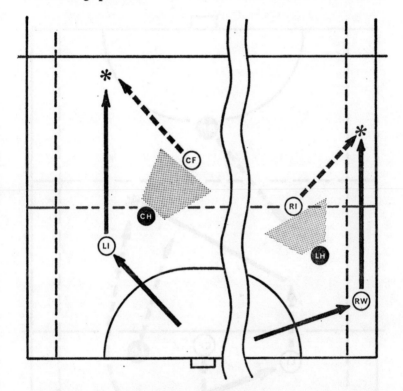

Fig. 51. The use of the straight pass. The shaded part shows the areas marked by the C.H. and L.H. respectively

(2) The use of the Straight Pass (Fig. 51). The most important point is that you should place exactly the right speed on the ball so that it gets to the correct spot at the same moment as he player.

Inner to Inner Passing. The consequence of inter-passing between the inners is to be seen in the counter actions of the opposing backs.

They are forced to change their covering and marking positions according to the position of the ball so that if it moves from one side of the field to the other, the back who was in a covering position should move out to challenge her opponent whilst the other back returns to cover. Two points are important in accomplishing the inner-to-inner pass successfully:

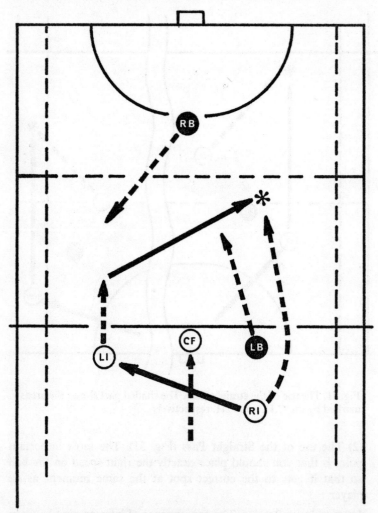

Fig. 52. Inner to inner passing. Notice the careful timing and accuracy in order to split the defence

Plate 13. R. W. Centring across the Circle. (*D. Arkell, England*). The opposing L.H. has been left behind and is making a hopeful attempt to intercept the ball with a reversed stick.

Plate 14. Receiving the ball from the right. (*V. Robinson, England*). In order that the stick should face the ball—the left side of the body is well forward and the left hand shows a strong control of the stick. V. Crombie (*Scotland*) is preparing to make a lunge tackle and watching for her opportunity very carefully.

(1) The Timing. Too hasty passing and the backs will not bother to counter your move. Draw your opponent toward you, then time your pass to avoid her and place it conveniently to your other inner.

(2) The centre-forward is important in the manoeuvre because without her help the centre space will be blocked. The task is simple—avoid stopping passes that are intended for the inner, and, when necessary, draw the opposing centre-half away from intercepting range.

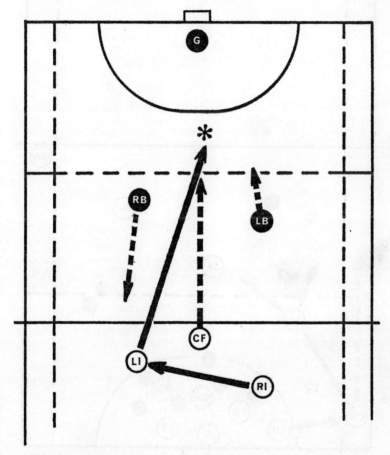

Fig. 53. Splitting the defence, as a result of the backs being caught square

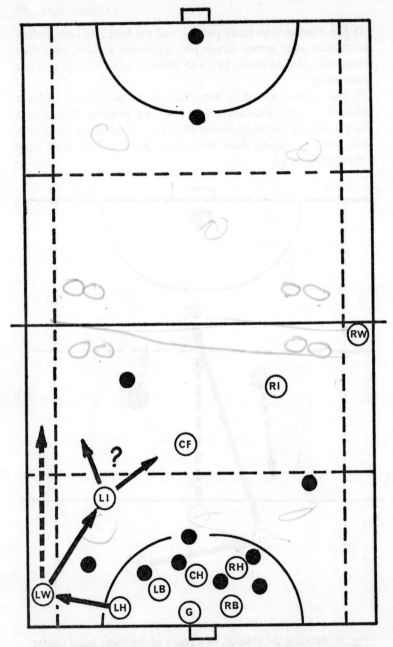

Fig. 54. The counter-attack. Players should anticipate the direction of attack and make ground in advance of the ball so that the passing movement can include a number of forward passes

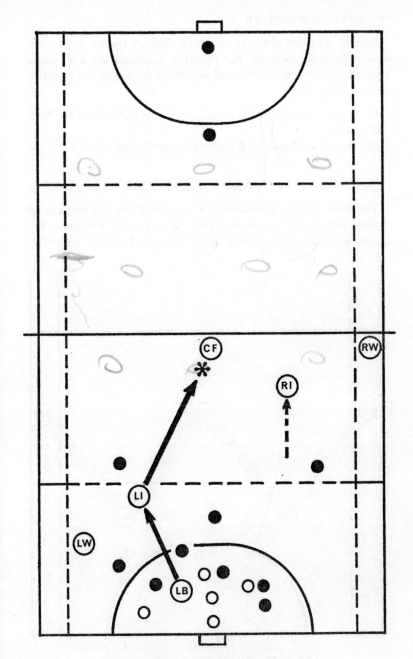

Fig. 55. Centre forward positioned up-field

Having prepared the way to break through the backs at their most vulnerable moment, the situation is poised for a decision. There are several possibilities of which the following are probably the most dangerous:

(1) Another timely 'inner-to-inner' pass angled behind the back (Fig. 52).
(2) The forward pass to the centre-forward (Fig. 53).

FORWARD FORMATIONS

The most effective positioning for a forward line is a well-spaced straight line as this formation makes the best use of the space. The speed of attack will depend upon the speed of the individual players.

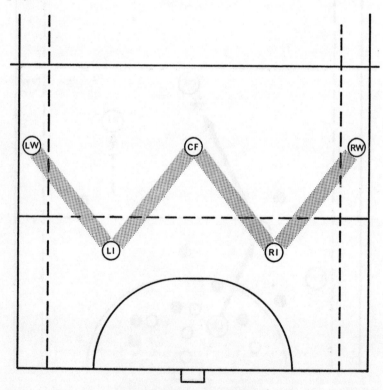

Fig. 56. The 'W' formation

A COUNTER-ATTACK PENETRATES MOST EFFECTIVELY IF IT IS LAUNCHED AS QUICKLY AS POSSIBLE (Fig. 54).

Another useful formation is initiated by the centre-forward positioning herself up-field together with the wing and/or inner farthest from the ball so that there is a formidable forward attack (Fig. 55).

Under pressure, it is necessary that some of the forwards drop back to help the defence (Fig. 56) and very often it is the inners who find themselves in defence, giving rise to the 'W' formation. Again, if the forward pass is made quickly and accurately, its advantage lies in the speed of the counter-attack.

N.B. In becoming absorbed with attacking formations, do not forget the possibilities of being OFFSIDE.

Do not be content with these suggestions, there are many varieties of passing movements with which to experiment; the more original the idea, the greater the element of surprise.

7 Match Play

MATCHES

To take a personal pride in preparing your kit indicates conscientiousness, enthusiasm and a player with high personal standards both on and off the field. A team that has clean boots and socks, clean well-pressed shorts and blouses makes a good impression and often seems to play better hockey than an untidy team.

Arrive in good time so that preparations need not be rushed. Each player prepares herself both mentally and physically in her own way—the worst atmosphere is created by the nervous player who by talking loudly of her nerves gradually affects others. Most people suffer from a degree of nerves but most people have the good sense to keep it to themselves. The quicker you can get out on to the field the happier you will feel, and gain confidence from the fact that you have been selected to play because the selection committee feel that you are the right person for the job.

The quickest way to pull a muscle is to start a match cold and stiff. Have some practice runs to loosen up and do a few stickwork exercises to get your eye in. If you are giving your goalkeeper some practice shots, do not completely demoralise her by scoring with every shot. She too, needs to feel confident that she is 'seeing' the ball well. After the match, do not stand around and get cold again. (Track suits are a great boon on these occasions.)

It is a mistake to go into a match with too many preconceived ideas of how you intend to play. Be alive to the possibilities but do not let the ideas dictate your whole game—you may find it depressing when you fail to get the opportunities simply because the situations never arise.

Once play starts, the team that takes its opportunities will win, so concentrate on creating those opportunities. Good concentration is an essential weapon in playing intelligently and being sufficiently flexible to adapt one's game to the opposition's strengths and weaknesses. Supporters can be distracting, so train yourself to ignore their encouragements, listen only for the whistle and any instructions or words of encouragement that your captain makes. Do remember that it is the privilege and duty of the captain to comment where necessary during the game; there is nothing worse than playing in a team in which everybody shouts at each other. A strong team is a unit because it has practised together and has been coached to have confidence in each other's ability and decisions. An experienced guiding word here and there from the captain should be designed to help the team produce its best play. Use the opportunity of half-time positively to discuss tactics for the second half.

Players who expect success to come easily are soon disillusioned on facing strong opposition. A determination and will to win ensures a player never giving up until the final whistle. If you are bounding with energy when it blows, you had better consider why —was it laziness on your part, the fact that the team has been too individual, or was the opposition very weak? When the match is over, remember to thank both the umpire and your opponents who have made the game possible, and do not forget to help to clear up. For your own peace of mind remember that players have 'on' and 'off' days and learn to take both the rough and the smooth. Having experienced a 'bad patch' you will know the feeling of a lack of confidence so do be appreciative of other people's feelings after a match—building confidence amongst each other will go a long way in contributing to a team's success. Lengthy post-mortems tend to destroy confidence, as, for the most part, the faults of the match are discussed. My advice is to recall the good memories and leave the criticisms until you can constructively use them as a basis from practice sessions or in furthering experience.

Coupled with the fun of playing matches comes the pleasure of meeting more people and making new friends. When the matches are 'at home', you are responsible for your guests' enjoyment. Extend to them the normal courtesies you would expect to show in entertaining a visitor in your own home. Arrive in good time to see that everything is made ready, including refreshments, and check that the changing rooms are tidy and ready to be occupied. Be on hand to welcome their arrival and see that they have everything they need—including some practice balls. After the match, when everybody has changed, it is usual for the hostesses to show their guests to the place of refreshment and take the opportunity to socialise. It is very disappointing and embarrassing to see teams rudely rush to sit down at a table to be together regardless of their counterparts. Certainly some of the younger teams will at first tend to be shy and not find it easy, but with experience, they will soon add to the usual noisy chatter. Having bid the opponents farewell, there only remains the washing up.

For 'away' matches you *should enjoy* the hospitality shown to you and in turn show your appreciation. If you find something lacking, be polite and refrain from making any comment. How often have you heard somebody complaining perhaps about your lack of showers, or offering tea and not cold drinks, or lemons rather than oranges? It certainly will not make a good relationship. Playing should be enjoyable, and matches are an opportunity to pit your wits and skills against other teams. It is the 'moment of truth' and whether you win or lose, meet it graciously. In winning, remember that an undisciplined exuberance can be embarrassing; and in defeat, show appreciation to the better team and let us hope that it will stimulate you into improving your game and being more determined to win next time. Above all, do not show any ill-will or bad grace—your captain will not tolerate it. I have known outstanding players dropped from their team on the grounds of bad sportsmanship.

With:

(1) Good stickwork at top speed.
(2) Keen anticipation, timing and judgment.
(3) A sense of positioning.
(4) Adaptability to meet changing situations.
(5) Patience and persistence and stamina to continue trying even in the face of difficulties.
(6) Confidence in each other which breeds individual confidence.
(7) Tactical scheming.
(8) A lively enthusiasm.

think what a team you would be.

TOURNAMENTS

Tournament play has a distinct character of its own and players should *concentrate* all their resourcefulness to make the most of every opportunity to score. Teams should be fit, fast and aggressive, determined to get to the ball first, and in obtaining possession 'sharpen' their own skills and timing to use it efficiently and effectively in the brief time available. Some teams waste so much time in taking free hits, rolls, corners, etc., that it is surprising that any goals are scored. Therefore, instil a sense of urgency, be alert, move quickly, and aim to keep the ball in play as much as possible. Familiarise yourselves with the scoring system in operation—in the event of a tie if the next consideration is corners, do all you can to prevent giving any away (goalkeepers note most particularly).

Tournament matches can become very hectic and confused, particularly in the circle. Try to maintain an open game with the backs and halves making a particular effort to swing the ball from wing to wing. On reaching the circle, a strong half-back line-up in support of their forwards will help to exert pressure, so will forwards who tackle back. Penalty corners are a wonderful opportunity to score and should be practised over and over again. If taken well, they are virtually 'a free shot at goal'.

Do not relax your grip for a moment—you have only got to give your maximum effort for a brief time before you can rest again, so whatever your position you can all contribute to the most positive target: SCORING GOALS.

GROUND AND WEATHER CONDITIONS

These can play a major part in the success or failure of match play. Before deciding upon tactics for a match—do give careful consideration to the ground conditions.

On a perfect pitch you can expect to play hockey at its best. The ball will run fast and true giving every opportunity for enterprising movements demanding accuracy and timing. Pattern play becomes a delight to watch and the tacticians are in their element.

On a hard bumpy pitch, the task of stopping the ball and general accuracy becomes chancy unless the players learn to watch the ball very closely. Take particular care when hitting the ball that the weight is well over the front foot to lessen the possibility of it popping up into the air (any error in technique will tend to show up on the poorer surfaces). Balls in the air are a hazard of bumpy grounds, and it is advisable that every player should be practised in bringing such balls vertically down to the ground with the hand.

Deep and early covering is essential in view of the possibility of missing the ball; this will enable you to have longer time in which to see the ball. In attack, this is a useful point to exploit on the opposing defence, i.e. to threaten the covering player with a speedy follow-up. Incidentally, in fielding the ball, make a special effort to keep the ball away from your feet so that you are not penalised for kicking every time you miss the ball with your stick.

On a wet muddy ground the ball must be hit (or kicked by the goalkeeper) much harder if it is to make the same pace as on a good pitch. Pushes are, more often than not, useless as they do not travel far enough. As the speed of the ball is likely to be slow, players should come to meet the ball, otherwise the opposition will have a gay time intercepting all the passes. Changing direction on a slippery surface will be easier for those with smaller strides, and also bear in mind that muddy grounds are tiring, particularly for those players who cover a lot of ground.

Weather conditions are less predictable, and are liable to 'blow up' at a moment's notice. Then the team that has its back to the adverse weather has the obvious advantage. (A weather prophet is a useful person to have in a team.)

The adaptation of skill and tactics to suit the ground and overhead conditions is a secret of a consistently successful team.

FITNESS

Fitness is the concern of both players and coaches. It will sharpen mental dexterity as well as physical performance and is as essential to individual athletes as it is to members of a team—perhaps even more so, as in an individual sport you are the only person affected by lack of stamina; in a team game, you have a responsibility to the rest of the team.

In a normal school curriculum, achieving and maintaining fitness should not be difficult, particularly if team players take every opportunity to join in the strenuous activities. Both hockey and netball lessons together with team practices form a good basis. Swimming is an excellent aid to general physical well being and squash and badminton will help speed reactions and train a keen eye.

The real test comes in the last ten minutes of a match—if you have not sufficient stamina to keep up with the pace of the game, or lack of energy causes your stickwork to become careless, additional fitness training is advisable. It is also advisable for any particular occasion when the pace is likely to be faster and play more demanding, for example—Junior County matches, Tournaments, etc.

Circuit training measures increasing effort against the time factor, it is a simple way of increasing stamina and improves both muscle tone and lung capacity. Special facilities in which to perform the exercises are not required, a small space should suffice. In the beginning, the exercises should be simple but carefully prepared so as not to overwork the same group of muscles consecutively. It should be arranged to incorporate the following:

(1) General warm-up.
(2) Exercising the abdominal muscles.
(3) Strengthening the leg muscles.
(4) Strengthening the upper limbs, particularly the wrists.
(5) Exercise the back extensor muscles.
(6) General mobility.

Having decided upon the particular exercices, there are two different ways of conducting a circuit:

(1) Each exercise has to be done for a certain length of time. As the performer improves upon the number of times the exercise is completed within the given time, so the length of the time is increased.
(2) Each exercise has to be completed a certain number of times and the time taken over all is noted. With every performance the time taken should be shorter.

The number of times a circuit is to be performed should depend upon the individual requirements. As the player's fitness increases, progress either the degree of difficulty of each exercise or the number of circuits. Exercises are generally made more difficult by:

(1) Increasing the resistance, either own body or otherwise.
(2) Increasing the height, whichever is applicable.

These are two specimen circuits.

BASIC SCHEME	PROGRESSION

(A) General warm-up: 200 skips or 200 runs on the spot.

As before.

(B) 10 Sit-ups.
Starting position—lie on back with feet hooked under something firm or heavy, put hands behind the head; rise into sitting position and touch knees with elbows and lower again to the floor.

As before—but with either the arms held straight above the head or, to make it more difficult, in addition hold a small weight, i.e. book.

(C) 30 Step-ups.
Step on to a chair or bench and down again, one foot after the other, extending the knees fully each time. Change leading leg after 15 times.

Increase the height of the chair or bench.

(D) 20 Finger 'press-aways'.
Starting position: stand about one yard away from a wall. Fall forwards on to your fingers until your head almost touches the wall then push away strongly to resume the upright position. Do not alter the position of your feet.

Move your feet farther away from the wall. If this is still too easy, progress to 'Press Ups' on the finger tips from a front lying position.

(E) 10 Back arches.
Starting position: lie on your front, hook feet under something firm or heavy and put hands behind the head. Raise head and shoulders off the floor backwards as far as possible and lower again.

Same exercise but stretch the arms above the head.

(F) 7 Squat jumps.
From a standing crouch position Stretch jump as high as you can and return to the crouch position to touch the floor. Emphasize the use of the arms to attain full height.

Hold a weight.

(G) 5 Wrist winders.
For this, a simple piece of apparatus is necessary. Obtain a short piece of splinterless wood, attach a piece of string, at the other end tie on a heavy object. Hold the wood at arm's length and wind the weight up as far as possible—then unwind slowly.

Increase the weight of the object.

(H) 10 Burpees.
From standing, drop to the crouch position with hands placed on the floor, with both feet together, shoot the legs out backwards as far as possible to land on the toes and bounce back into the crouch position, then to standing.

Increase the number of times.

N.B. It is unnecessary to repeat the warm-up between each circuit.

CAPTAINCY

Captaincy is an exciting honour guaranteed to thrill any hockey player, but it is no easy task to be responsible for your team both on and off the field. Any captain worth her title should remember that her responsibilities do not begin with the first whistle, particularly in school. In authority the captain is the physical education teacher's right hand and the liaison between her and the team. There are many occasions when it is necessary to act upon your own initiative and assist in the running of both team and departmental affairs—a good captain should be able to recognise these opportunities and act efficiently and promptly. Do delegate some of your duties otherwise you will be kept very busy—besides, it is important that other people should know what is involved and feel part of the organisation. Troubles, grumbles, etc., cause discontent and need sorting out promptly—some will be petty, others well founded and your job is to sift them through and act upon their seriousness. Occasionally it is necessary to discipline a member of the team, which is no pleasant task, therefore, it is essential that one's own example is beyond reproach.

Be concerned with the courtesy, behaviour and personal appearance of your team—low standards undermine team relationships. Keep an eye on players who are shy and find it difficult to be good hostesses, see that they enjoy their opportunities and are not left out. Confidence, both individual and in each other, breeds team spirit, so assess matches constructively and aid team morale with encouragement. Your experience will be invaluable during matches, and the team will look to you for advice, and incidentally respect you for the way in which you give it. No player likes to be 'yelled' at nor told what to do at every opportunity.

In some games 'the toss' can be a very important factor in winning or losing matches. It can be no easy choice to decide which way to play first, and, in your mind, you must weigh up:

(1) The conditions: overhead, underfoot and possible slope, the glare of the sun, a tiring wind, a waterlogged circle, etc.

(2) Your goalkeeper's preference. It would be a foolish captain who did not consult her last line of defence as to what would suit her best.

(3) Your team's psychological and physiological approach to match play. For example: some teams are poor starters and it is best to give the forwards the best conditions in the second half; others aim to score a goal in the first thirty seconds and need the good conditions to score first. Stamina-wise, some teams are suspect and are best advised to play downhill in the second half. Some waterlogged circles cut up so badly that, by the second half, individual skill becomes hopeless.

Make an opportunity for the team to gather together briefly just before the start of a march—to focus their method of approach to winning the game. At the back of your mind, you should have an idea who to ask to take the penalty bully should it arise. Now that the forwards have lost their '25-yard bully' practice, members of the defence could feature in this art if they are prepared to practise. A suitable temperament is vital as it is quite an ordeal—and some experienced captains who have the right philosophical approach decide to take it themselves.

With the end of the match, thrill or disappointment can make one forgetful of courtesies. Remember to thank both the opposing captain and your opponent as well as the umpires, and to express your appreciation for any aspect that has been particularly pleasing.

There may be occasions when you disagree with a decision; having made your point to those concerned do not dwell on it. Seeds of discontent have a habit of growing out of hand. Tact is an essential quality particularly in gaining co-operation, and, by showing appreciation, impromptu help may be forthcoming next time.

Taking on the responsibilities of captaincy can be detrimental to a player's personal standard. For the most part, it is caused by unselfishly diverting concentration from herself to the members of her team. Give thought to both aspects, but bear in mind that if your own loss of form means that you yourself are unable to carry out the instructions you give to your team, it is high time you concentrated less on the others and more on your own play.

Do not weigh up the success of your captaincy with the success of the team—the continuing enthusiasm and sense of enjoyment shown by the players is a better indication.

JUNIOR TO INTERNATIONAL

The annual International held at Wembley Stadium in March is probably known to most readers even if only on television. Perhaps you enjoy being part of the vast throng and experience the feeling of great excitement on seeing the two teams emerge from the dark tunnel. Has it ever occurred to you that one day you could be down there in the middle of the arena playing for your own country? Many of those international players were once spectators experiencing the same thrill of occasion. They began their hockey careers representing their school XI and a number of them probably played for their junior county teams up to the age of eighteen. From junior level, the talented players progressed via a club to their senior county or area teams. Remember, selectors are always on the look-out for young talent. Following a series of county matches, divisional or territorial teams are selected, and from those matches emerge the final International team. Even then, competition doesn't end, as once in every four years all the hockey-playing countries meet for an international tournament. Over the last twenty years The International Federation of Women's Hockey Associations has held its Conference and Tournament in South Africa, England, Australia, Holland, U.S.A. and Germany. You could be on the first rung of the ladder to an international career. Success will not come easily (anything worth having never does), so take every opportunity to learn more about the game.

Each season, somewhere amongst the many school First XI players, are the internationals of the future.

Part Two

Part Two

8 Teaching/Coaching

There seems to me to be only a slender line dividing the two—
teaching is a fundamental necessity to learning—coaching follows
in getting the best from an individual or team.

A good coach knows her subject thoroughly and is able to express
it effectively. A sense of humour, ingenuity and patience together
with an infectious enthusiasm will stimulate interest in her subject.
Her leadership, example and ability to assess play will reflect in
her teams and her handling of individual temperaments may spell
success or disaster.

Coaching is based on observation—and observation can be made
easier with good organisation. Games are simpler to coach if both
teams wear positional bibs, failing that, crossed bands for the
attack, single bands for defence. In setting up practices, aid your
observation by indicating clearly the way everybody should play.
Large classes should be well disciplined and responsible girls should
take turns to umpire. Create a routine in both preparing and clearing up after games lessons, train the captain to be alive to her
responsibilities, and the class sufficiently observant and helpful to
carry out the requirements. A purposeful atmosphere will discourage time wasting. Some sessions are best planned to begin with
stick work, progressing to the game, others to start with the game,
and later breaking it down to practise obvious weaknesses in the
play.

Skills are more readily developed in a game situation. (In progressing skills, introduce their game context as soon as possible
with interim practices where necessary, i.e. The technique; passive
followed by active opposition). Practices always involve a combination of skills, but do achieve a standard in your original object
before turning to another aspect. (The standard of 'the other aspect'
will be a good guide to your progress.)

Coaching a game can be done in three ways:

(1) The coach having complete control of the game—stopping it when she will. (Suitable for tactical coaching.)

(2) Umpires controlling the game whilst the coach moves round to coach individual players. (Particularly helpful for individual coaching and positioning.)

(3) The coach critically observing short umpired match conditioned games. (Useful for coaching match analysis.)

'Just playing' is seldom of value to anybody. Outline your purpose and follow it through. However, do not be too rigid in your programme, for the mood of a class may suggest that your plans are doomed from the start. Never feel guilty in deviating from your intention, provided the class has gained from your doing so; much of the best coaching is developed spontaneously. By the end of a session, it is desirable that *every* member of the group should have learned something new or improved something old, so select and plan the dominant theme, carefully relating the group's ability to the degree of difficulty. It is always easier to develop a simple idea than to go backwards from a task that has proven too difficult. Because you have taught a particular detail, do not assume that it has been learnt.

There is little value in giving a long complicated practice to a group of second years whose energies are frustrated in the preparations.

It is also advisable to consider the weather, for it can have a strong influence on the lesson's success. On windy days, it is difficult to make oneself heard; on warm days, too much early activity can sap the energy from the game; on bitterly cold days, brains as well as fingers become numb, and a muddy day in the depths of winter is not the best day for teaching pushes and flicks.

Good footwork is the essence of good hockey and even international players will practise their footwork. Girls of all ages should be given plenty of exercises designed to improve the major game skills. Practices should include: changing direction, pivoting, altering the length of stride, accelerating, swerving, side-stepping and abrupt halting. These exercises should be executed correctly first without the ball, and then worked up to top speed with the ball.

From the very first time of picking up a stick, players should be encouraged to discover the best technique for themselves. This discovery, carefully directed by the coach, should not take up any more time than the old rigid 'do this, do that' teaching technique.

In training players to assess match play critically, begin the very first lesson by teaching how to observe. Develop the group's natural interest in answering the 'hows' and 'when' and 'wheres', and programme practices to help each other. It is surprising how astute even young children can become. Direct the increasing experiehce to stimulate tactical discussions, and before long, half-time will be the signal for a general exchange of observations quite worthy for basing play for the second half.

A syllabus can be a snare and a delusion. Used correctly, it is a handy guide for coaches, particularly where there is likelihood of staff changes or visiting coaches. However, it does not cater for the flexibility demanded in teaching hockey through the years. It tends to bind the coach to a rigid play regardless of the weather conditions and the various speeds of learning. Most teachers prefer to develop techniques as they arise and need scope for preferential practice. Modern teaching methods encourage informality and experimentation as a means of achieving results, but hockey is governed by rules which in turn formulate good style. This, together with the limiting time factor, means that teaching points have to be carefully directed—N.B. not imposed). Do not completely discard informality and experimentation, for although games have not the same scope as gymnastics or dancing, their use helps to promote initiative, freedom for ideas and constructive individual discipline.

The All-England Women's Hockey Association organises a coaching qualification scheme at two levels—Elementary and Advanced—for the purpose of 'promoting a high standard of coaching throughout the counties, with a view to encouraging enthusiasm, individual initiative and a sense of achievement amongst players'. Coaching courses are run by the Association, and candidates wishing to take the test should make individual application to their County Associations.

COACHING BEGINNERS
Aim:

(1) To arouse interest and enthusiasm.
(2) To appreciate the advantages of skill and teamwork.
(3) To learn the basic techniques as quickly as possible and enable game participation.

In the first year, most coaches find themselves covering very much the same detail though not necessarily in the same order. My approach is a suggestion on which to base individual methods.

Every lesson should find the group learning something new, and that includes general background as well as rules and skills. It is unusual for beginners never to have seen hockey played, and most will know what a bully involves, but the technical jargon can be overwhelming and should be explained as the sessions proceed, as should the rules. By the time the beginners are ready for their first game, they should have a simple working knowledge and expect to be penalised for the obvious infringements. Do explain to the players that this can be a problem for the coach as there are occasions when she wants the game to flow without interruption for kicking, etc., and is prepared to ignore the minor mistakes.

Too much practice and not enough competition will quickly dampen early enthusiasm. The lesson's climax should be competitive in some form, and the life one can inject into a group of beginners on incorporating the goal circle into the practices never ceases to amaze me. This awareness of the goal at an early stage is an important lead up to attacking play in the first full games.

In order to achieve quick and neat footwork, the coach should plan her sessions to contain footwork practices and observe carefully to see that a satisfactory standard is reached before continuing the session. In the early stages, it is of paramount importance to be particular over the details, and this will save a tremendous amount of revision. Pick your points clearly and stress them by introducing them in different contexts, or by referring back to other experiences.

One of the first questions often asked concerns left-handed hockey sticks. This is a good opportunity to explain why a left-hander has such an advantage in hockey, and the need for the right-hander to strengthen her left wrist. From the very first session, I encourage the girls to run and hold the stick with the left hand at the top, believing that it encourages a stronger left wrist and better advanced technique. Stress that the right hand is put on to the stick when strength or force is required.

The development from the first lesson to the first full game should be carefully planned and organised so that the time between the two is as short as possible.

Suggested programme: (Approximately 50 minutes)

Session 1

(1) Advise on selection of communal sticks if necessary.

(2) Immediately introduce and explain three infringements of the rules—sticks, kicking, hitting with the rounded side of the stick.

(3) Practise the running action.

(4) Learn to carry and run with the stick in the left hand, trying not to inhibit the running action. (The quicker the stick is carried easily and comfortably the better.)

(5) Give a ball to each person and ask them 'to move with it' as fast as possible.

(6) Encourage class participation in directing the style to achieve what *you* want (the grip, ball close to stick).

(7) Hitting—describe it as a swinging action—and remind the players of the rule concerning raised sticks and of the dangers of breaking it.

(8) Introduce the idea of passing by moving with a partner, hitting to each other. Stress the position of the ball; that if the passing is accurate, neither of the partners should ever stop; the angle of the swing of the stick.

(9) The bully, and when it occurs in the game. Point out the starting position and that the left shoulder points toward the direction you want to go.

(10) Demonstrate the importance of speed on the ball after the third strike, and the pulling of the ball away from the opponent's stick.

(All the way through the lesson take the opportunity to familiarise players with any hockey expressions or rules that crop up.) Passing is closely allied to dribbling, and it is very important that a seemingly minor detail be strictly adhered to—that is the change of grip from dribbling (hands apart) to passing (hands together) to receiving (hands apart)

Session 2

(1) Question group as to the rules learnt last time.

(2) Individually move with a ball reminding them of the grip (if necessary).

(3) Explain and demonstrate simple obstruction, and the ways to avoid it. Teach running round to the left of the ball emphasising quick footwork. General practice.

(4) Practise hitting in fours—positioned in a square. Drive the ball in a clockwise direction emphasising: position of the ball, a straight follow-through for accuracy, elimination of 'sticks'.

(5) Passing in more detail. (Be sure that the players are gripping the sticks correctly and that they change the grip for the different techniques.) In twos, arrange inner-to-wing passing practice. For the player on the left, it is important for her to keep on the left side of the ball, and if chasing it, exaggerate the lead of the left side in an effort to keep the ball on the field. For the player on the right, it is important for her to turn her stick toward the on-coming ball, otherwise it will glance off and shoot away to the right. (This idea should be developed when you concentrate on learning to receive the ball.)

(6) Bully practice on the 25-yard or centre lines; reminder of the techniques of pulling the ball and show the futility of 'hacking' at each other's sticks. Later, add an incentive—in order to score a goal, the ball should cross the centre of 25-yard line; naturally, each tries to stop the other.

Session 3

(1) Repeat moving the balls stressing the importance of the left hand and keeping the ball away from the feet. Divide group into two teams for the purpose of both competition and observation of each other.

(2) Using half fields: running, then racing with a ball and shooting a goal, stressing:

   (i) shooting as soon as the circle line is crossed
   (ii) not to stop the feet in order to shoot (and reminding of the change of grip where necessary).

(3) Driving in twos, concentrating on the speed of the swing and hitting the ball with the middle of the stick. Demonstrations to include the importance of the head over the ball and a strong left arm (plus the revision of other details that might crop up).

(4) Two teams—left wing passing to left inner. Revision of: position of the ball, keeping moving and achieving such accurate passing that by superior speed the pair ahead can be overtaken.

Discuss what happens, and the different techniques involved when reaching the end of the field and turning to play the other way, i.e. left wing becomes right wing and left inner become right inner.

(5) Bullies on centre line running the length of the field in order to score a goal. The contest should be cancelled the moment any player breaks one of the four rules that they have learnt.

(6) Following a very active session, this is an opportunity to stop a little early in order to discuss general matters concerning hockey in school and beyond. School team supporters are always welcome, and it is a great advantage for beginners to see a game being played before going into a full game themselves.

Session 4

(1) Divide into two teams. Combine dribbling with shooting, in racing to shoot goals. (Discuss taking aim and the strength of the shot.)

(2) Driving in threes positioned to form a triangle, encourage the feet to move around the ball and as little pause as possible between the stopping and hitting.

(3) Receiving the ball, demonstrate the importance of 'giving' on catching a hard ball and liken the same action to the stick receiving a hockey ball.

(4) Continue in threes, with one 'rolling' the ball to the next who concentrates on receiving the ball to stop stationary.

(5) Introduce the 'rolling' technique and its context and continue with the practice.

(6) Running and passing in twos, insisting on turning the face of the stick to meet the oncoming ball. A third player starts the passing movement as would a half-back and follows up behind (the introduction of the first idea of the role of the defender and the attacker).

(7) Three v. three (2 forwards, 1 defence). Organise small pitches with goals and demonstrate the game with an 'able group'. Insist that the rules be kept (as far as possible) and explain the role of the defence player and point out the value of space. It is sensible for the players to be easily identified as forwards and defence—single bands and crossed bands are simple to arrange. If time, 'take a deep breath' and organise the whole class.

The next session should be arranged to stress defence play and introduce the simple principles of tackling. Creating an interest in defence play should ensure a fairly workable proportion of defence players to forwards when it comes to the three-aside games.

According to the group's progress, gradually increase the size of the games and choose practices in context so that the players can understand and transfer their new skills to situations in their games. Never hesitate to revise past work in your effort to attain good technique.

In planning your early sessions, it saves time to consider numbers in each practice and arrange a simple build-up. You will have noticed that whereas the first session was predominantly individual work, the second was in twos and fours, and the fourth session was for threes and sizes. Within this build-up, beginners can start to appreciate team work and by the game stage should *know* the value of teamwork.

At some point, the weather will prevent play and the wise coach should have several schemes in readiness to use the time constructively.

Learning to keep goal always appeals and, with indoor space, it is an ideal opportunity to introduce it to everybody. No doubt, space will be cramped and numbers will need careful organising, but it is a useful occasion to train the players to check up on each other's technique.

Start with explanation of equipment, use of stick and positioning and clearing. Everybody can practise with tennis balls and no pads (in order to move freely); progress to pads and indoor hockey balls with the rest of the group practising shooting. The very next outdoor session be sure to include goalkeepers in the practices and, if equipment allows, it is often a good idea to allocate two to a goal, so that when there are moments of inactivity, they can keep each other occupied with practices.

Field lines, team names and positions have to be taught, so too, the understanding of what happens when the ball goes off the boundary lines.

Choose the day for the game wisely—a high wind, or a bitterly cold day can ruin all your careful preparations. When the weather is particularly cold and frustrating and I am ready for the first game, I have had success with introducing a modified session of football. The group never lacks for enthusiasm or activity and I find that I can build up the idea of positioning and teamwork together with a working knowledge of corners, rolls, etc. On resuming with hockey sticks, etc., the game flows surprisingly rapidly, and with a little help from the coach in distributing the ball, most 'standing around' is cut to the minimum. Polo balls encourage the game to flow, as beginners find the lighter ball easier to hit.

Having achieved a satisfactory first game, do not be too disconcerted when everybody wishes to try a different position. Although the pattern will be temporarily upset, if you keep key players in their familiar positions, the game will quickly resume its normal flow and the 'key' players can change next time.

The players respect a coach with high standards and will be more conscientious in their own individual approach to practising. The better the foundations are laid at this stage, the easier and more enjoyable your efforts will be to stimulate good play later.

ELEMENTARY COACHING

Aims:

To maintain interest and enthusiasm.

To increase individual skills.

To become tactics conscious.

To take a sense of pride in good execution.

By now, the natural games players will be showing their abilities, and those having difficulties will be obvious. To make a general improvement in standard, even the weakest player must develop her own game, whilst the talented must be stretched to satisfy her resources. Hearty enthusiasm, whilst carrying some along, has the opposite effect on the unenthusiastic; a genuine individual interest will arouse much more effort.

Some class games lack flow and it often reflects too much dependence on the coach; although it is easier to have learner umpires, every girl should know the rules well enough to resume the game correctly after any infringement, so that, if necessary, the coach can give her undivided attention to a player.

Reverse stick play is an integral part of hockey techniques and coaches should make the opportunity to teach it properly. Its effectiveness depends upon both its efficiency and the element of surprise within a game situation. There is a danger of its leading to lazy footwork and obstruction, particularly when it is self taught. An individual's footwork can suffer if it is taught too early—wait until the players can appreciate its values and have the basis of good footwork and skill with the stick, then start teaching the simple movements.

Having attained a certain degree of proficiency in the basic technique, stimulate new interest by introducing tactics. Many players become absorbed with new ideas and see a new purpose to learning skills. The opportunities at corners, rolls and in circle play take on fresh importance.

Keep an eye on the 'fringe' players. Under no circumstances allow the goalkeeper to feel cold and left out, otherwise your enthusiasts will quickly lose interest and change to another position.

Suggestions:

(1) Organise an 'extra' to give the goalkeeper practice when the game is at the other end of the field.
(2) Play a game with the sole purpose of showing concentration and good positioning, (remember to check progress constantly).
(3) Set up corners and goalkeeping situations.

When a goal is scored, give a moment to the goalkeeper, either in discussion or arranging several practice clears whilst the players reform for the bully.

Wings also quickly lose interest if the game loses its flow, so be prepared to step in and play yourself, in order to distribute the ball; or switch the game, if you have no stick, by suddenly picking up the ball and rolling it in a different direction.

Change inners who do not pass to their wings, and insist that the backs adopt a method of covering right from their first game; if they are not well occupied they will soon resort to idle chatter.

I have already mentioned the importance of having the ball positioned correctly before passing to the right or left; in addition, it is necessary to be able to hit the ball when the weight is on either foot. The acquiring of this skill is the responsibility of the coach, for to mention it to a class sometimes ends with girls 'tying themselves into knots' in an effort to discover their own shortcomings. If the coach takes the trouble to observe her players, it is soon plain which player always prepares to pass or shoot with the favourite foot forward, and a practice at this point will prevent any interruption to the flow of a player's game.

TEAM COACHING

To represent the School's First XI is the aim of all aspiring hockey players. In order to achieve a good standard in the First XI, there should be younger teams as a training ground for the ultimate achievement. Most schools run a Second XI as well as a Junior team; but before introducing a very young team, one must weigh up the consequences of introducing match play too early. Once satisfied that the team will maintain a constructive method of play, and that the opposition has the same ideal—match play will be fun and worth while.

Regular team practices are essential and unfortunately this is not as simple as it sounds. Dinner hours are not really sufficiently long, and strenuous activity is not advisable directly after a meal. Some schools, whose pupils have travelling problems, agree to practices within school hours, otherwise the best time is after school. No pupil should be exempt from participating in after-school activities by reason of travelling difficulties. Seek co-operation from the Head, and if physical education has its rightful place in school life, help will be available.

At the beginning of the season, gather together the real enthusiasts and form the practice squads, making it quite clear that once they become members, you expect complete reliability in attending practices. Personally, I do not encourage the half-hearted enthusiast, for, in my experience, sooner or later, she will let you and the team down. I would rather coach the less talented to the best of her ability knowing that it gives her a tremendous pleasure to represent the school. In forming a practice squad of approximately twenty-four for each team, and in the senior school, the combined First and Second XI forming the nucleus, it is then up to the coach's ingenuity to keep the whole group's interest and enthusiasm throughout the season. (How easy it is to blow hot or cold according to the whims of the weather.) As the season progresses, give the various deserving members of the squad a chance to show what they can do in match play; you may be pleasantly surprised. A school's strength is to be found not in their First XI, but in the ability of the reserves, and by choosing a squad system, you have the opportunity to build a strong tradition for the game within the school.

Every team has its strengths as well as its weaknesses, the less of the latter the better, so use the enthusiasm of the season's opening to eradicate some of them; at the same time, present some new material to stimulate fresh ideas and better technique. At senior team level, 'teaching' as such should be over, and with a view to getting the best out of each player and moulding a team, coaching in its true sense should take its place.

There are several considerations in assessing a team:

(a) Physical: speed, stamina, tenacity.
(b) Mental: a practical intelligence.
(c) Psychological; determination, courage and a will to win.
(d) Degree of proficiency in individual stickwork, teamwork, positional play.

In making such an analysis, do not forget individual temperaments, for in the final reckoning, this could be the most important aspect of all.

In the light of your analysis, prepare the training programme to include:

Stickwork practices
Planned tactics
The development of individual skill
Increased stamina
Exercises for good footwork
The elements of surprise and enterprise

Prevent the possibility of staleness by interspersing practices with other aspects of the game, e.g.:

Umpiring sessions
Instructional films
Voluntary sessions with positional changes
Seven-aside or indoor hockey
Matches under tournament conditions
Inter-team potted sports.

For stimulating new ideas and fresh enthusiasm, support a Territorial or International match.

Practice games can be organised in several ways:

Team v. reserves
Team forwards and defence reserves v. forward reserves and team defence.

Forwards and halves reserves v. reserves, team backs and goal-keeper

or the teams can be divided according to the particular team work or tactics.

Where to start? Usually my first aim of the season and one which occurs over and over again wrapped in different disguises is 'meeting the ball'. To gain and keep possession is to dictate the pattern of play and to get to the ball first involves gathering or intercepting the ball whilst accelerating or running at top speed. *Keeping* possession is the natural development.

With interchanging, players need to experience other positions and the relative theory of technique and when to use them, and I spend a considerable time in playing team members out of their usual positions. Experiencing the opposite position presents an insight into playing their own.

To aid match play, pressure training, competitive practices and game situations will add a degree of urgency and may throw light upon the varying temperaments within the team. The team whose coach knows of and can handle the psychological idiosyncrasies, particularly under stress, and who senses the right moments to be discreet, critical or enthusiastic, is indeed fortunate.

MATCH PLAY

To have prior information as to the strengths and weaknesses of the opposition can be useful, but do train teams to 'play as they find'. Teams can expect to meet such varying standards and styles that scheming observation and flexibility are qualities of an adaptable and successful team. To warn of possible strengths is to aid anticipation. Once the match begins, the coach becomes a bystander and is obliged to watch the fruits of her labours. The captain takes over the leadership and it is to her that the team looks for advice and encouragement. This emphasises the importance of a close co-operation between the captain and the coach.

After all the excitements, resist holding fanatical post-mortems. Players need to unwind and this is the moment to recall the good points and build confidence and enthusiasm to play even better in the next match. The constructive criticism can be the basis for the next practice.

TEAM SELECTION

In some schools the coach prefers to do her own selecting—in others the selection committee consists of the captain, vice-captain and coach. It is never an easy task to choose, particularly where enthusiastic juniors or your friends are concerned. However, it has to be done, so put aside the personal element, try to be scrupulously fair and let justice be seen to be done.

Look for the signs of a skilful player, i.e. ball and body control, speed, anticipation, concentration, intelligence, determination and the ability to execute skills at top speed.

Trials are never a very satisfactory method of team selection, but schools are fortunate in that the committee has more opportunity to get to know the players both on and off the field and is not committed to select a team for the whole season. If it is made clear that teams will be selected for each match according to the current form this helps to obviate the disappointment of being dropped. It also makes it possible to select a different combination better suited to cope with the particular set of circumstances. Obviously, some players will be outstanding and 'select themselves'. Others need to be observed astutely both with the ball and without it. It is with these closer decisions that the committee system is more effective in that players can often spot a strength or weakness amongst themselves not obvious to the coach. In choosing between two players, take into consideration: their ability to distribute the ball, tenacity, adaptability, and see how they fit into the team situation playing against the same opponent. There is a saying that 'you can only play as well as your opponent allows'.

The eleven most outstanding players do not necessarily form the best team—some are too individual or spasmodic with their effort to combine together effectively. Other less obvious players who distribute the ball wisely can contribute far more to the team's success. It is unlikely that your selected eleven will fall neatly into their respective positions. In re-assigning positions, the selection committee should judge each situation on its merits; some will argue that the best players are probably the most adaptable. Whatever the arguments, the committee should back its decision confidently until the next selection when, in the light of the previous match, the situation is reviewed. Having watched a player many times, be fair and

Plate 15. The author—Carol Bryant—shows the result of a body swerve and a quick acceleration in moving into the circle leaving the tackler to chase behind.

Plate 16. Note the use of the left arm in bringing the ball under control. Meanwhile the G.K. is advancing quickly in order to narrow the angle. (*D. Parry, England. H. Flockhart, Scotland*).

take care not to be too previous with your assessment, she may have overcome your past criticisms.

All players seem to suffer from loss of form—the cause is not always clear and nobody knows how long it will last, least of all the player herself. According to the individual temperament, it is best treated with a patient encouragement through the bad patch, by a change of position, or a complete lay-off. In choosing a travelling reserve, adaptation is the first consideration.

Although it is difficult to generalise, briefly, I look for the following specialist attributes in selecting a school First XI:

Goalkeeper   Concentration, agility, a good eye, a strong construc- tive clearer of the ball, and the sort of temperament not to be upset by letting in a goal.

Right Back   Courage and timing, sufficient speed to run the extra distance necessary to 'cover' adequately.

Left Back   Skill on non-stick side, courage and timing, 'a feel' for playing on the left.

Right Half   A good pivot and pass to the right, speed to cover deeply, stamina to be tenacious.

Centre-Half   Speed and stamina, tenacity, a quick hit to the right and left whilst on the run, quick recovery. A good team player.

Left Half   Quick footwork, ability to get round the ball, a power- ful hit.

Right Wing   A good right dodge, hard centre.

Right Inner   Constructive distributor, accurate shooter, an ability to make an occasional individual effort. A good swerve.

Centre-Forward   Speed, enterprise, good acceleration, body swerve and neat stickwork, a good eye, a 'ball hunter'.

Left Inner   Scheming distributor, a team player. A good scorer.

Left Wing   A feel for playing on the left and particular speed to get round the ball and centre hard.

Team selecting can be a fascinating and rewarding pleasure. On the other hand, it can be a thankless and much criticised job, particularly when the team results are disappointing. However, take courage, re-assess the situation, give thought to new combinations and try again.

COACHING/UMPIRING

It is most important to correlate coaching with the rules at every opportunity; therefore, you should be thoroughly conversant with the 'rules' and coach the skills in close conjunction and be quick to spot and correct any tendency to foul.

It is helpful to be aware of some of the possible pitfalls, so consider the following:

Tackling. The correct technique is evolved to avoid any form of obstruction so that the tackler should not impede her opponent's movements or stick in attempting to play the ball. So often the tackler becomes careless and allows herself to bump into her opponent, or plays her opponent's stick instead of the ball.

Dodging. Again, there should be no body contact which could lead to obstruction. Therefore it is necessary to coach a good body swerve, particularly when using the right dodge and to avoid putting the ball on to the legs of an opponent.

Receiving. In stopping the ball, it is advisable to keep it away from the feet (so too in DRIBBLING) in an effort to lessen the chance of kicking the ball. Therefore, stress the importance of extending the left elbow in an effort to play the ball farther away from your feet.

Hitting. The technique of hitting is governed by the fact that the stick must not be raised above shoulder level and the ball must be hit with the flat face of the stick. In order to prevent 'undercutting' the ball, stress the importance of having the head over it at the moment of striking and to follow through smoothly. Though the hit should be powerful, remind the players that if they hit an opponent at close range, they must expect the umpire to award a free hit against them for dangerous play.

Passing. Some players in an effort to get their feet round the ball to pass to the right, prevent a tackle by interposing their shoulder or even body between their opponent and the ball. In this case, it is necessary that the player should achieve a quick pivot to pass to the right.

The use of the Reverse Stick. Encourage players to keep the ball well ahead of themselves so that other players have access to a tackle. Once the ball is played near the feet, the shoulder often obstructs the challenger.

In coaching tactics, do ensure that the players are all aware of the Obstruction and Offside rules. The main stumbling block is often the third-party obstruction. Frequently it is only the obstructed player together with the umpire who realises what has occurred, i.e. a player puts herself between an opponent and the ball whilst another member of her team clears or plays the ball. The situation is more likely to occur when space is minimal, so the goalkeeper is more likely to be involved in third-party decisions; in fact, some situations can lead to a penalty bully.

Though the coach should train players to avoid fouling, umpires need never fear redundancy—ground conditions, fatigue and the less-well-coached players will always present plenty to do.

COACHING DEVELOPMENTS

The use of the reverse stick must be encouraged. The moment of teaching the skill should be chosen carefully, for it should never be a substitute for good footwork, but be a method of:

(1) guarding the space to the left side of the body,
(2) initiating sudden changes of direction.

On the Continent, the men influence (if not coach) the style of play, and the reverse stick and playing to keep possession of the ball are widely used. This tends to reduce the flow we come to expect from the English style, as the passing tends to be more square. By taking the good points from both styles, the South Africans are leading the way to developing first-class hockey.

There is a danger of causing obstructions, possibly because of the women's weaker wrists, and therefore it is essential to coach reverse stick play carefully, relating it to good footwork and the obstruction rule.

The influence of football is an interesting development. New ideas in formations are already being tried but the consequences involve more time for team practices. School is an ideal situation to experiment—though not to the extent of jeopardising a player's chance for team selections outside school. Again, I stress the importance of flexibility.

Interchanging in an effort to wrong-foot the opposition could be developed into a more fluid operation. It is an attempt momentarily to confuse and demands a high degree of teamwork to ensure complete understanding amongst the operators. Interchange positions sideways as well as forward and back, so that wings can play inside forwards, wing halves play backs, and defence play forwards, etc. This flexibility can only be achieved with intelligent, adaptable and skilful enthusiasts who realise the opportunities this tactic affords.

Keeping possession of the ball is a method of slowing the pace of the game, and in attack involves the use of the half-back line in preparing to strike for goal. The square pass and the back pass are the obvious weapons, and should be practised to obtain a high standard of efficiency and accuracy.

MATCH ADMINISTRATION

In planning to play matches against other schools, administrative work is necessary. Girls enjoy taking responsibility and this is a good opportunity to show their organising ability. Obviously, the physical education staff bear the ultimate responsibility, therefore it is important to supervise the arrangements.

The fixture list should be made in good time, remembering the fixed dates of the annual tournaments. Matches should be regular without being too demanding; the first and last weekends of a term are usually unsatisfactory due to lack of practice or end-of-term functions. A steady build-up of strong matches increases confidence. A hard match prior to a tournament helps to 'sharpen' a team's play.

Display the fixture list prominently so that the players may take note of the dates, and in the week previous to a home match, confirm the fixture and make the final arrangements concerning the starting time and possible cancellation. Cancellation should only be necessary when it is raining (or snowing) or when the pitches are too wet or too hard. I add the last, not only for safety, but because I feel that frost-bound pitches are not conducive to good hockey at Junior level.

Having agreed a fixture for several teams, it is the duty of the person in charge to organise an umpire for each team. Lone umpires are detrimental to match standards and too many schools arrive for matches understaffed. There are remedies: do not organise so many matches (quality rather than quantity), stagger the starts, train schoolgirl umpires, interest other members of the staff in umpiring. This responsibility toward umpiring should be taken seriously. A conscientious umpire should keep herself up to date with all changes in rules, and when unsure of the interpretation of the more complicated rules, seek advice or arrange to attend courses. County associations frequently organise courses aimed particularly at helping school and club umpires.

Seek the co-operation of both the groundsman and the caretaker for home matches, so that all is prepared, ensure the equipment is in good condition and do not forget to check on the arrangements for oranges and refreshments.

For away matches, make the necessary travelling arrangements and be sure that you know the exact destination.

It is not unreasonable for schools to levy a match fee of 6d. on each player in order to help defray the costs of refreshments, coach travel etc.

The social training, to my mind, is the most important aspect of inter-school matches. The spirit in which the game is played, the friendliness extended by both sides, the common courtesies shown, stem from the person in charge. The greatest compliment an opposing team can pay is to acknowledge how much they enjoy playing you.

Have you considered arranging a real climax to the season? It creates keen interest and raises the prestige of the game within school. Junior hockey is developing so rapidly, not only in the Home Countries but also on the Continent, that the opportunities of exchange visits are tremendously exciting. The preliminary contacts are sometimes difficult, but an advertisement in *The Hockey Field* (c/o The Deanery, Bampton, Oxon.) or an enquiry to the A.E.W.H.A. offices could be productive.

INDOOR HOCKEY

Indoor hockey is increasing in popularity as the number of sports halls, and large indoor areas, become available. So much so, that the All-England Women's Hockey Association have included a special set of rules at the back of their Rules publication.

Usually teams consist of 6 or 7 aside but this largely depends upon the space available. The minimum space is considered to be 30 yards by 15 yards—however, I have managed in smaller areas by reducing the number of players. In some halls it is possible to include the walls into the playing area and this adds more skill and fun to the game.

The equipment should include flat rubber-soled shoes, suitable studless kickers for the goalkeeper, and a specially designed ball called a 'pudding ball' obtainable from the larger sports firms. Where damage to either the stick or the floor seems possible, it is advisable to cover the stick with a sock, or pad it with tape and sponge rubber.

Indoor hockey is fast even though the space is confined. It requires proficient stickwork together with a high degree of accuracy. It is not permissable to hit the ball, only push or flick, but not to a height exceeding twelve inches, therefore it is necessary to be able to both push and flick strongly and accurately. Owing to the speed of the indoor surface, it is better to use the push to pass, and the flick as a shot or a method of getting yourself out of difficulty, so that the flight of the ball deceives the eye. Dodges should be particularly neat and well timed, and tackling should be positive as opposed to negative; with space at a minimum, the defence must seize the initiative and rely on good timing to win the ball.

Team formations depend on the number of players:

Seven-aside: Players are best organised with goalkeeper, two backs, link half and three forwards.

Six-aside: Goalkeeper, two defence players working to a covering system, three forwards ready to adapt to half-backs when under pressure.

Five-aside: Goalkeeper, a covering back, link half and two forwards.

Teamwork is essential and the organisation within a team should be particularly flexible—forwards should be prepared to drop back into the defence when under pressure and the defence should be ready to attack.

Tactics: Interchanging helps to create space, so long as the rest of the team reorganises quickly to take advantage of the momentary surprise.

A passing movement which includes a pass across the width of the playing area opens up the game. It is particularly advantageous if given early, as it forces the opposing defence to move, leaving more space in an otherwise limited area, in which the forwards can manoeuvre.

Try to keep possession of the ball amongst the team; short push passes to the free player are probably the easiest way, as the floor surface lends itself to accuracy in controlling the ball.

Take the trouble to learn to play off the wall, as it is possible both to beat an opponent and pass to a member of your own team, particularly on finding yourself in a cramped situation. Strengthen your flick and push to come off the wall quickly.

The goalkeeper is often the most agile member of the team in indoor hockey, because the ball moves very fast, and she has little time to see it and react. It is probable that she will be very busy, and if she can manage to make her clearances constructive, the forwards can counterattack with great speed. At corners, she is at a distinct disadvantage if the shooter has a powerful flick. In these circumstances, it is vital that, as the corner is taken, she should note the ball's direction, and quickly spring forward to narrow the angle for the impending shot.

Indoor hockey is usually run on tournament lines, and when played well is a very satisfying game.

Should it sound interesting to you, I suggest you obtain a copy of the *Rules Book* as printed by the A.E.W.H.A. and try it yourselves.

9 Umpiring

This chapter is written with a view to helping the learner umpire, and also the physical education teacher in school.

Essential Equipment

(1) Current book of rules.
(2) A whistle on cord.
(3) Score card and two pencils.
(4) Watch with seconds hand or stop watch.

Do wear clothes in which you can run comfortably and keep warm. At the same time wear colours different from the teams and wear studded shoes to help keep you upright.

Theoretical requirements

(1) *Thorough knowledge of the rules.* One of the most satisfactory methods of assessing your knowledge is to take the 'C' test, and to do this apply to your County Umpiring Secretary (the address will be found in the A.E.W.H.A. Handbook). Refer to the *Code of Rules for the Game of Hockey* as authorised by the Women's International Hockey Rules Board together with *The Guide to Umpires and Notes of the Code of Rules* and *the All-England Women's Hockey Association Notes for umpires and players.* Also included are the rules for five- and seven-aside hockey, indoor hockey, simplified rules for use in junior schools.
The Rules are obtainable from: The A.E.W.H.A., 45 Doughty St., London W.C.1.
(2) *Know the duties of the umpire.* It is the umpire's responsibility to see that:

(a) The field is marked accurately.
(b) The flag posts are correctly positioned.

(c) The goal cages are correctly constructed and inspect the goal netting with a critical eye to see that it is securely fastened to posts. You would be in an embarrassing position, having awarded a goal, to discover later that the ball went through

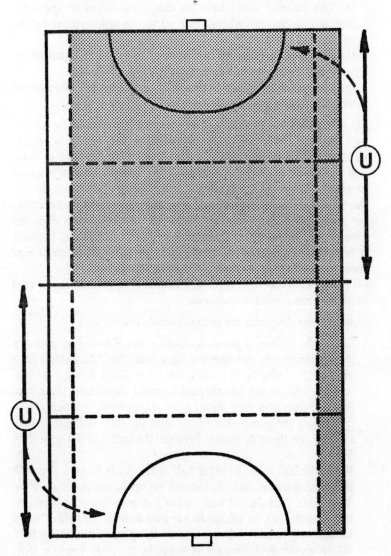

Fig. 57. The Umpires' territory

a hole or gap in the side netting. A piece of string in your pocket could be a useful accessory.

(d) The balls are leather. (Plastic balls may only be used on agreement by the two captains.)

(e) The players' sticks have no dangerous edges or splinters, and advise players where their sticks do not confirm to the rules.

(f) No sharp articles be worn by players—metal badges or brooches come into this category.

(g) Players uniforms are in line with the rules—i.e. short shorts and short socks are illegal.

(3) *The Umpire's Territory.* Each umpire is expected to umpire half the field; from the centre to goal line, that which is on her right when she stands on the centre line facing the field of play, and the whole of the near side line. The umpires generally agree to give decisions in the complete tram-line area on their side of the field. It is a mistake to stipulate the areas too dogmatically, for a few occasions do arise when the umpire on the opposite side should be prepared to blow her whistle. However, beware! it is normally regarded as a breach of umpiring etiquette if you blow in your other umpire's half of the field (Fig. 57).

(4) *Positioning during the game.* Consistent re-positioning is vital to giving correct offside decisions.

(N.B. In some diagrams the second umpire is omitted.)

(a) *At the start of a game,* position yourself on a line with the third defence—in this case the right half (Fig. 58). Should your view of the bully be obscured, alter your angle to view it comfortably but do not be tempted to stand on or near the centre line, for then you may miss an offside by being left behind.

(b) *During the game*—keep level with the third defence so long as there are three defenders between the ball and the goal (Fig. 59).

When the ball is in the other half again, position on a line with the third defence, but should she be up in attack beyond the centre line, you should wait on the half-way line—and remember, nobody can be offside in her own half of the field. Do not be tempted to move down toward the play in the other half. When giving decisions about fouls in the tram lines, a clear signal should suffice, failing that, use your voice.

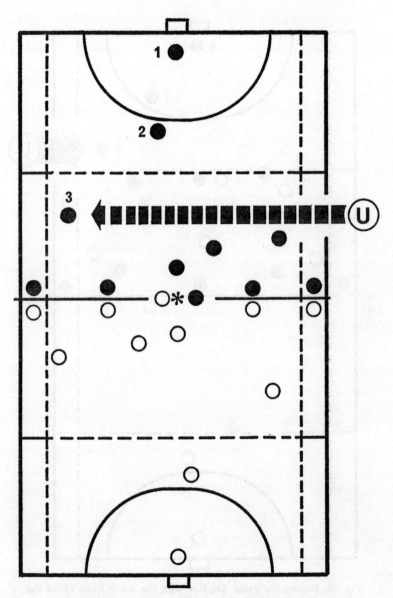

Fig. 58. The Umpire's position at the start of the game

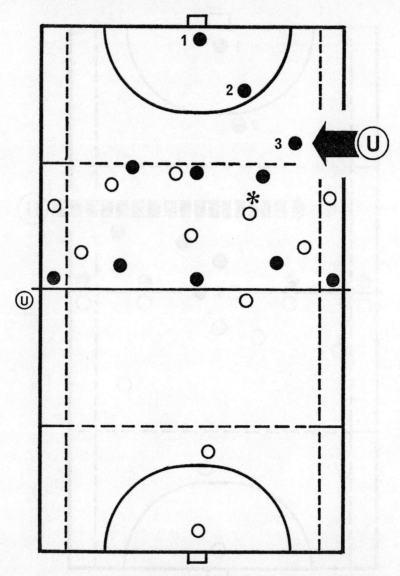

Fig. 59. During the game. On line with the 3rd defence whilst the
other umpire waits at the half-way line

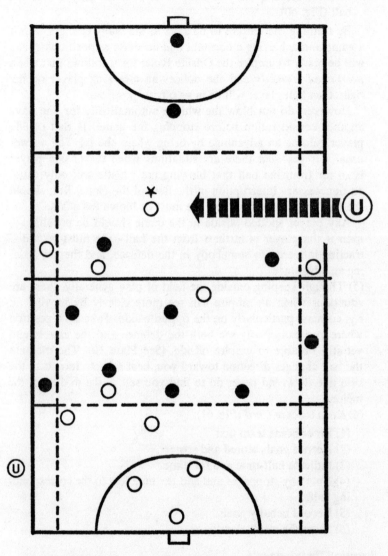

Fig. 60. The breakaway, showing the umpire on line with the player with the ball

(c) On the occasions the forwards break through past the third defence, move quickly to keep level with the player with the ball (Fig. 60).

By training the umpire to be alert to the many changes within a game and achieving a constant and accurate re-positioning, she will be ready to umpire the Offside Rule; for it follows that when *positioned correctly* and she notices an attacking player on her right, then that player will be in an offside position.

However, do not blow the whistle automatically for you have another consideration before stopping the game. Is that offside player gaining an advantage by being where she is? The answer usually is yes—*but* there are situations when the offside player is so far from the ball that blowing the whistle will only cause an unnecessary interruption in the flow of the game. But, should the ball be directed near her, she must be blown for offside.

Any player spotted offside in the circle should be penalised— even if the player is farthest from the ball—she must be a distracting influence to somebody in the defence, and thereby gaining an advantage.

(5) Though keeping outside the field of play generally, there are situations when an umpire can see more clearly by moving in, e.g. corners, particularly on the opposite side. Take up a position where you can clearly see both the defence and the attack, and yet still be able to umpire offside. (See Plate 10). The moment the ball changes direction toward you, beat a hasty retreat to the side line. It would never do to find yourself in the middle of the mêlée.

(6) *Keep a Score Card* (Fig. 61).

(1) Enter home team first.

(2) Record goals scored and scorers.

(3) Indicate half-time and full-time.

(4) Note any stoppages and add the time lost to the corresponding half.

(5) Record penalty goals.

(6) Show the result clearly.

Practical Requirements

To umpire competently is to handle the game fairly and for the enjoyment of all those taking part. In addition to a sound theoretical foundation:

(i) The manner should be calm and confident.

(ii) The whistle should be blown firmly—although not so fiercely as to intimidate the players.

(iii) Arm signals should be given promptly. In raising your right arm to shoulder level you are indicating to the team playing in that direction that you have awarded them a free hit or roll, and vice versa with the left arm. On the whole, there should be

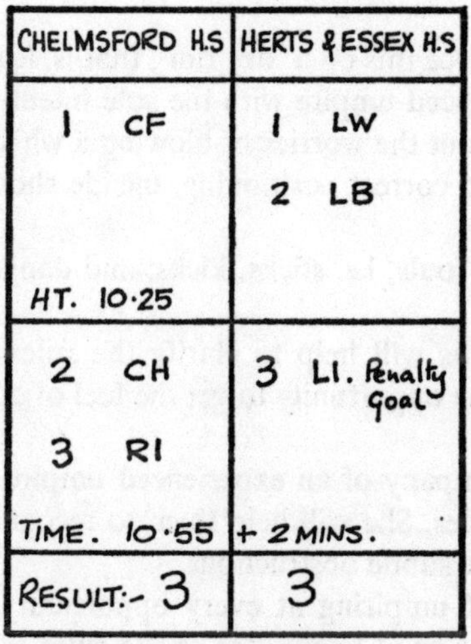

CHELMSFORD H.S	HERTS & ESSEX H.S
1 CF	1 LW
	2 LB
HT. 10·25	
2 CH	3 LI. Penalty goal
3 RI	
TIME. 10·55	+ 2 MINS.
RESULT:- 3	3

Fig. 61. Score card

no need to use two arms. Only occasionally is it necessary to indicate to the players the exact spot the ball is to be placed or rolled in.

(iv) In addition to signals, use the voice to award corners, rolls, and hit outs and to clarify any confusion.

(v) Dissociate yourself from any loyalties.

(vi) Acquire a constant concentration throughout the game, one lapse at the crucial moment could be disastrous. Try to be oblivious of all distractions, particularly in matches and tournament play, when a complete isolation is imperative. When the game moves to the other end of the field, beware of becoming a spectator—keep your umpiring vigil even when you can relax from the immediate play.

(vii) Umpires do make mistakes (so do players) but do not allow yourself to be put off the task on hand by worrying over an error.

Training Umpires in School

(1) Encourage an interest in umpiring almost from the very beginning.

(2) Arrange for interested girls to be prepared and take the 'C' test. At the end of this chapter a sample 'C' Test paper is reproduced.

(3) Practise whistle blowing, arm signals and use of voice for rolls, corners, hit outs.

(4) Teach positioning—introduce this on a 'dry run', that is, learn by moving behind an experienced umpire with the sole intention of practising positioning without the worries of blowing a whistle and controlling the game with correct positioning, offside should be obvious.

(5) Start umpiring the simple fouls, i.e. sticks, kicks, and dangerous play.

(6) Try umpiring corners. This will help to clarify the rules in the umpire's mind and give the opportunity to get the feel of controlling a game.

(7) Watch a match in the company of an experienced umpire to advise or discuss points of rules. She will help them to recognise fouls and particularly the more subtle obstructions.

(8) Encourage the practice of umpiring at every opportunity. I cannot stress too strongly that good knowledge of the rules is as important as good stickwork, and especially to members of the First XI.

(9) Try to attend an umpiring course.

Having passed the 'C' Test, girls should be encouraged to umpire inter-form, house, school and tournament matches. In my opinion, it is a fallacy that schoolgirls are not strong enough to umpire school or tournament matches. Provided they are coached individually and finally vetted, their acute sense of fair play will show them to be every bit as good as the average adult umpire.

Umpiring Etiquette

The umpire of the home team is expected to act as hostess. It is usual for her to invite the visiting umpire to choose which side of the field she would like to umpire, and between them to decide who is going to time which half. Half-time is an opportunity to confer

Plate 17. The L.I. (*D. Parry, England*) having broken through the defence to be faced with the G.K. moving towards her, is faced with a quick decision. What would you do? (She scored with a quick flick placing the ball to the G.K.'s non stick side).

Plate 18. A tense dual (*D. Parry, East v. T. Martin, S. Africa, G.K.*). The interest of this situation lies in the two nearest players. Alongside the shooter is a free forward—but maybe she has seen a space past the G.K. Alongside the G.K. and almost impeding her is another member of the defence. Has the G.K. called so that she is getting out of the way—or might she deflect the shot into the goal?

and discuss any points of play or umpiring that may have arisen. At the end of the match, do compare scores, it is not unknown for umpires to differ.

Umpiring at Tournaments

Tournaments which demand an outright winner and require the umpires to record the number of corners awarded can be a problem. Obviously, a goal is a clear-cut score, and many umpires prefer to hold their whistle in the circle in the hope that the forwards may turn the foul into a goal. However, in this instance, it is possible for that team to fail not only to score but fail also in the final positioning, owing to a poor record of penalty corners. In my opinion, it is only the very experienced umpire who can play the advantage rule, and for the rest of us, we must be very tight on umpiring circle play and be prepared to award penalty corners promptly. After that, it is up to the players to learn to score from corners—after all they are supposed to be to their advantage!

Umpires should be alive to the fact that tournament play can become wildly enthusiastic and can rapidly get out of control. Therefore, it is important that they should handle the game firmly and not be intimidated by the players, spectators or the situation itself. It is not unknown for an umpire to warn a team or a player for dangerous play or rudeness, but, thanks to the spirit in which women play the game, it is most unusual for a player to be sent off the field.

The two most important rules and ones on which to base the whole approach to umpiring concern Offside and Obstruction.

Rule 11. Offside

In being able to quote the rule, and knowing the correct positioning to umpire it, you have only to put it into practice.

There are players who look furiously at the umpire who penalises them for offside—forgetting that it is not for 'being offside' when you receive the ball, but being offside at the moment *the ball was hit or rolled in* that counts. In some sports a player can be put 'onside', this cannot be in hockey, and any player *gaining an advantage* by being offside should be penalised. A forward who rushes the goalkeeper can be 'offside', but so long as she is making an effort to reposition correctly and is in no way impeding the defence, she should not be penalised. In another instance, a forward who, nearing the back line, makes a back pass, leaving herself in an 'offside' position, should not be penalised so long as she does not remain there and become a distracting influence to the defence. Players who run off the back line to avoid being offside should choose the moment to return so that they do not affect the game by running through an offside position.

Rule 12. Obstruction

Interference with sticks is, as a general rule, very badly umpired. Any player who is prevented from playing the ball by having her stick held, hooked or interfered with in any way should be penalised. 'Hacking and stick trailing' are stick obstructions and often appear to be accidental; however, they are signs of lack of control, laziness or failing stamina, and lead to dangerous play so should not be tolerated.

No player may unfairly prevent another from playing the ball. 'Turning' is recognised by most, but the more subtle obstructions are not easy to spot, though players will recognise the occasions more easily, having had first-hand experience.

Umpiring Less Skilled Games

Sometimes I find myself officiating at a match that appears to be all fouls—and I wonder where to start. The situation is often caused by teams lacking any form of teamwork, who follow the ball wherever it goes. These are the occasions when I feel for the sake of everybody's enjoyment and safety that the umpire must become a coach—to point out the futility of muddling and the value of passing to players positioned in the spaces. Once the game begins to flow, umpiring becomes possible.

In games involving younger players, or those of less ability, again the game must flow to be enjoyable and it is not easy to decide which infringements to penalise. I start with the simple fouls that players should know, i.e. sticks, kicking, turning, and then progress to hitting each other's sticks and anything leading to dangerous play, if necessary, teaching it as the game progresses. On no occasion would I allow a goal to be scored from an offside position.

More Advanced Umpiring

Observant umpires will notice how, in attempting to keep possession, some players ward off an adjacent tackler by turning slightly away. Under these circumstances, the tackler is helpless.

Third-party obstruction. One player prevents another from playing the ball whilst another member of the team gains possession of the ball. More often than not, the prevention is a bodily obstruction or shielding action, although you should be on the look-out for the held stick version. The right dodge often leads to third-party obstruction and requires careful umpiring. For instance: A right inner executes a right dodge around the left back who, on getting in the way, prevents the right inner from playing the ball whilst the left half moves in to play the ball.

12 (c) The interpretation of *dangerous play* prompts much discussion, but it is agreed that dangerous play is relative to the situation and speed of the ball. An undercut is obvious, the player will have her weight on her back foot and the blade of the stick uppermost. A ball accidentally rising into the air perhaps off a bump in the ground is an instance which no rule governs, although the players will be relieved to see it brought down; nobody enjoys playing a missile hurtling through the air. Players who, by using their hand, bring the ball back on to the ground are doing the game a service.

Disregard any player who kicks or carries forward a ball that is hit or kicked at them *from close range*. Penalise the player who played the ball initially for dangerous play. No stipulation is made as to the distance between the two, the umpire must use her common sense and decide whether or not the player had time to take avoiding action.

At corners, the forwards have no right of way in shooting. The defence have a hazardous task in moving forward to tackle, and it is expected that the forwards should not shoot directly into the legs of the defence at *close range*, but show consideration in skilfully avoiding them. When a corner is hit hard and quickly, the defence have less time to make ground, and should have time to see the path of the ball.

Under the same interpretation, a goalkeeper must not be allowed to clear into the air if it is dangerous to the incoming forwards. A dangerous clear is considered to be so when either:

(i) the goalkeeper's weight is back so that the ball tends to fly up, or

(ii) the clear is directed straight at an oncoming forward who has no time to get out of the way.

Be suspicious of frequent high-lifted balls into a closely packed circle, even if they are controlled—they are a source of danger, particularly for the players dealing with them. The follow-up may be:

(i) batting the ball in the air,

(ii) causing a defending player to lose time in bringing the ball down whilst the opposition wait for it to hit the ground and gain a brief time advantage.

Most flick and scoop shots at goal are not considered dangerous. It is a movement that requires both control and skill and the ball does not travel as fast as a drive.

Penalty Bullies

There are many more cases deserving a penalty bully than are awarded. Why is it that umpires seem loath to give them? Can it be that they are uncertain of the rule, or are they so poorly positioned that they do not see? A penalty bully is awarded *'when a goal most probably would have been scored if a foul had not occurred'.* More often than not, the ball is speeding toward the goal and is prevented from entering, e.g. player sits or lies on the ball; legs and feet in the way; a high ball saved by using the stick higher than shoulder level; shot saved by back of stick, etc.

Another occasion occurs when a defender attempts to save a goal by fouling the shooter.

A third-party obstruction can lead to a penalty bully—for example:

A forward shoots at goal from close quarters, the goalkeeper partially saves but the ball goes behind her toward the goal. The goalkeeper does not move so that the attacker is prevented from playing the ball whilst another defender moves in to clear the ball before it goes over the goal line.

Playing the Advantage Rule

Novice umpires should leave well alone and not attempt to hold the whistle until their experience is such that a quick assessment of the situation may show that the *effect* of the foul may be to the *advantage* of the opponents—in which case, allow the game to proceed. Too much whistle-holding by an inexperienced umpire can result in a deterioration in the standard of the game, and frustrated players.

Bad Conditions

Sometimes it is necessary for matches to be played in extreme conditions. In these circumstances, the umpire should temper her interpretation of the rules with the players' difficulties and remember that she can help everybody to make the best of a disappointing occasion. Sometimes weather conditions can deteriorate so badly that the umpire should take the initiative and halt the game to consult with the captains about the possibility of abandonment.

Indoor Hockey

The rules are set out at the back of the *Hockey Rules Book*. This is a fast and exacting game when the umpire requires a keen eye and a very quick reaction.

When the walls are included in the playing area, the umpire has a problem in avoiding the ball, and where facilities permit she often retires to a position where she can overlook the game.

Umpiring Qualifications

The All-England Women's Hockey Association presents three grades of register for umpires.

C. Register

In most cases this is both a theoretical and practical test and is run by the individual territories as a basis and an incentive to raising the general standard of umpiring.

Candidates must show knowledge of the rules, ability to whistle confidently, basic positioning, efficient signalling, ability to *control* a game satisfactorily, and be expected to umpire a good standard school or club match. Some counties make arrangements for the candidates to be watched by an experienced 'watcher', others require the candidate to umpire a minimum number of matches and ask the captains of the teams playing to sign the umpire's card. (A sample 'C' Test paper will be found at the end of this chapter.)

B. Register and Register for Men

Candidates are expected to be able to umpire senior county matches to the satisfaction of a panel of watchers set up by the Individual Territorial Umpiring Sub-Committees. They will be expected to show:

(1) correct positioning throughout a game.

(2) a positive but unobstructive manner in the handling of the game.

(3) a good understanding of the rules.

(4) and give correct decisions on the more subtle fouls, i.e. Off-side, Obstruction, etc.

A. Register

Having attained this grade, the umpire is qualified to umpire internationals as well as territorials. In addition to the qualities of a 'B' umpire—the 'A' umpire:

(1) is expected to show a very high standard and consistent interpretation of the rules.

(2) should be experienced in holding the whistle and playing the advantage rule

(3) must have quick mental reactions and physical speed, to allow her to keep pace with the faster game.

No umpire can achieve a good standard without patience, enthusiasm and a certain sense of humour. If you find umpiring enjoyable, then there is every possibility you will do it well. Good umpires are always in demand.

SAMPLE 'C' TEST PAPER

(1) What are the duties of the Captains as given in the Rules?

What courtesies should she pay to the umpires and the visiting team? (4 marks)

(2) Draw up a score card of a match between the Optimists and the Robins played on 4th November at 2.30 p.m., in which both teams scored once in the first half and the Robins once in the second half. The game was stopped for 2 minutes for injuries in the first half. (5 marks)

(3) The Rules show that there are three conditions under which a played cannot be offside. Name these.

Where should the umpire position herself to note
these conditions?   (6 marks)

(4) Give six points an umpire should look for when a
free hit is taken.   (6 marks)

(5) On what points regarding equipment must the
umpire be strict to ensure the safety of the players? (3 marks)

(6) On what two occasions may the scoop shot not be
used?   (2 marks)

(7) When do you award:

  (a) Penalty corner?
  (b) Penalty bully?
  (c) Where is the penalty corner taken?
  (d) Where is the penalty bully taken?   (4 marks)

(8) When and to whom is a roll-in awarded?

Where and how must the ball re-enter the field of
play?   (4 marks)

(9) What is the maximum time a game may be stopped
for an accident?

How is this lost time adjusted?

How is the game restarted?

What is the duty of the umpire to an injured
player?   (6 marks)

(10) Give decisions:

  (a) In stopping a ball at knee height, a player lifts
  the handle of the stick above her shoulder.
  (b) At a penalty bully, the attacker sends ball over
  the goal line (not between the posts).
  (c) Defending R.B. takes first time hit at ball, which
  rises into body of oncoming forward.
  (d) Blue L.B. kicks ball in the circle and ball goes
  straight to waiting Red R.I.
  (e) As Red C.F. dribbles ball, Blue C.H. attempts to
  tackle but Red C.F. turns her right shoulder and
  elbow to hold off the Blue C.H.
  (f) At corner, C.F. deflects ball to L.I. who takes
  first time shot.
  (g) R.I., with ball just outside circle, shoots at goal.

In attempting to stop shot, G.K. deflects ball into the net.

(h) L.I., in circle, makes good shot at goal, which is stopped by the G.K. C.F. rushes the shot but G.K. clears to R.I. C.F. remains near G.K. while R.I. shoots.

(i) In stopping a shot at goal, G.K. slips and drops her stick. She then kicks ball clear before picking up her stick. There are no forwards within striking distance.

(j) At a centre bully, the Blue L.I. crosses the line as soon as the bully starts.   (10 marks)

Reproduced by kind permission of the East Anglian Women's Hockey Umpires Sub-Committee.

10 Tournament Organisation

Many clubs and schools find themselves involved in running tournaments—sometimes for their own players, at other times for visiting teams. Since 1967, teams have been allowed to play for trophies and although this may not be new to junior players, it is an innovation to senior hockey and will probably lead to most tournaments being geared to a Final.

Stages of Organisation of an Outside Tournament:

(1) Appoint an organising committee.
(2) Decide on a date and obtain suitable grounds with adequate changing facilities, bearing in mind that the number of pitches will govern the playing time.
(3) Decide on entrance fee if running expenses are necessary.
(4) Notify all teams in the area mentioning:
    (a) Nature of tournament (11, 7 or 6 aside, indoor, etc.)
    (b) Date, place and time.
    (c) Entrance fee charge.
    (d) Closing date for application. (Give yourself approximately 2–3 weeks for organising.)
    (e) Numbers of teams and names of umpires. (Stress the importance of an umpire for each team.)
    (f) Ask for indication as to colour of uniforms.
    (g) Exchange telephone numbers in case of emergencies.
(5) After the closing date, call meeting of Organising Committee to discuss and arrange its duties.

Business:

(I) Decide whether or not to gear the tournament to a Final and Trophy.
(II) *If* the Final is to be played out—what considerations should

be made to govern the final decision should the score remain equal even after extra time.

(III) Depending on the number of entries and pitches available, arrange the number of sections (an equal number of sections will ease the organisation).

(IV) Make the draw, bearing in mind that seeding the stronger teams (or previous winners and runners-up) often ensures a more worthwhile final.

(V) In deciding length of matches, it is necessary to consider:

(a) The overall playing time.

(b) The number of teams within a section.

(c) Whether every team within a section will play each other.

(d) Whether to play the same time for the Quarter Final, Semi Final and Final.

Should the playing conditions warrant a change of ends half-way through, the absolute minimum time to ensure the games are worth while, is, in my opinion, 14 minutes (7 mins. each way with no pause at half-time)

(VI) Draw up a code of rules for deciding section winners. Suggested orders for considerations:

(a) *Points*. 2 for a win—1 for a draw. Some tournament organisers weight their wins more heavily, but this is a matter for individual preference. In my experience, the simplest is the best.

(b) *Goals*. To me, goals scored against are as important as goals scored for—so that I assess the goal record by taking from the total scored the number of goals scored *against*.

(c) *Penalty Corners*. Remember to make provision on the umpires' score card.

(d) *Long Corners*. Items (c) and (d) are not altogether satisfactory owing to the varying standards of the umpires. However, it is a way of determining the stronger team in the final count, so long as the umpires are aware that corners could be taken into consideration and umpire circle play strictly.

(VII) Arrange the umpires—preferably in the same section as their own team but umpiring different matches.

(VIII) Organise the recording of results. Either, appoint a steward for each section who carries the section's result card and records the results direct from the umpires, and sends them on to the score desk or, appoint runners to collect official umpires' cards immediately after each match, and take them back to the Official Scorer.

(IX) *Appoint Officials for the Day*

    (a) Organiser. It is wise to leave her completely free of duties in order to oversee the smooth running of the proceedings.

    (b) Scorer/Recorder.

    (c) Timekeeper.

    (d) Bellringer.

    (e) Stewards for each pitch or section.

    (f) Runners for: Organiser,
                      Recorder,
                      Stewards,

    (g) Refreshment organiser.

    (h) Overseer for umpires—who arrange the umpires for Semi-finals and Finals.

(X) Circularise all entrants and helpers giving *complete* details of the tournament, i.e. directions to the ground, programme, rules, number of balls required, etc. and the facilities available, i.e. showers, sale of refreshments, cancellation telephone number.

(XI) Complete the necessary paper work (Figs. 62, 63, 64).

Final Arrangements:

    (1) Detail officials of their responsibilities.

    (2) Request all helpers to be in good time.

    (3) Label the pitches, changing rooms and cloakrooms.

    (4) Check order of provisions for sale of refreshments.

    (5) If considered necessary, inform police of possible traffic congestion.

    (6) Arrange provision of medical aid.

    (7) Obtain distinguishing braids or bibs for matches involving identical teams and alert stewards.

    (8) Obtain bell or similar, plus pencils, rubbers, rulers, etc., for use at score desk.

    (9) Clear all areas of unnecessary objects.

    (10) Arrange presentation of awards (if necessary).

On the day: Stand back and enjoy the fruits of your labours. A good organiser is one who anticipates eventualities; co-ordinates the various aspects; delegates the individual responsibilities wisely, and is essentially calm.

SECTION I		TYRRELLS	BYRON	MILDMAY	HULTON	CHAPMAN	MARSH	PC LC	GOALS FOR GOALS AGST	WON	DRN	POINTS	POSITION
TYRRELLS	G PC LC												
BYRON	G PC LC												
MILDMAY	G PC LC												
HULTON	G PC LC												
CHAPMAN	G PC LC					W 0 1 3							
MARSH	G PC LC					L 2 1 2							

SECTION WINNER :—

Fig. 62. Result sheet

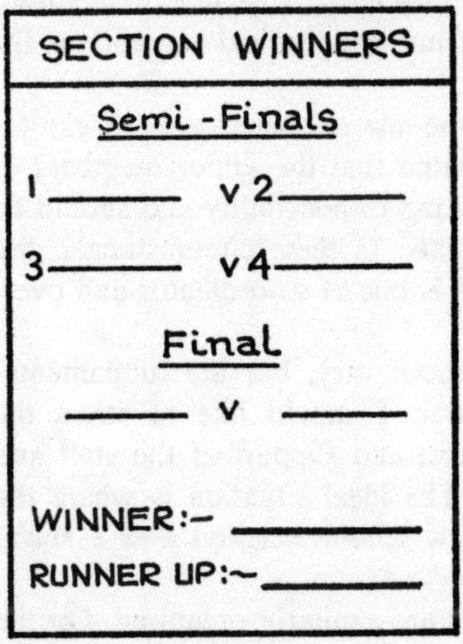

```
┌─────────────────────────┐
│  SECTION  WINNERS       │
│  ─────────────────────  │
│    Semi - Finals        │
│                         │
│  1_____  v 2_____ │
│                         │
│  3_____  v 4_____ │
│                         │
│        Final            │
│                         │
│  _____  v  _____  │
│                         │
│  WINNER:- _____  │
│                         │
│  RUNNER UP:- _____ │
│                         │
└─────────────────────────┘
```

Fig. 63. Winners

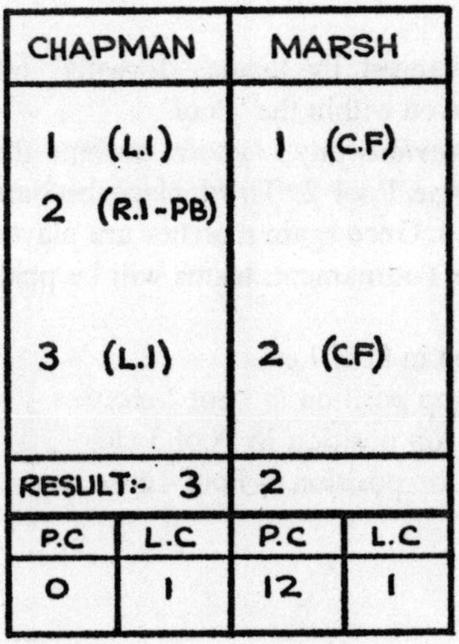

CHAPMAN	MARSH
1 (L.I)	1 (C.F)
2 (R.I-PB)	
3 (L.I)	2 (C.F)

RESULT:- 3	2

P.C	L.C	P.C	L.C
O	I	12	I

Fig. 64. Umpire's score card

After: Arrange general cleaning up, particularly litter; thank officials and helpers; letters of appreciation (the use of facilities, etc); file score sheets, all relevant information and suggestions for improvement ready for next time!

School Tournaments: Organise the internal tournament on similar lines to the external, bearing in mind that the senior members of the school are quite capable of taking responsibility and should be trained in the organisation of events. In these circumstances, the role of the physical education staff is one of co-ordinator and overseer.

Obviously, situations within school vary, but the fundamental arrangements are similar. However, I should like to stress the importance of obtaining the interest and support of the staff and inform them of relevant details. The ideal situation is where the hockey tournament is treated as a school function and a social training ground.

Variations: Not all tournaments are similarly organised. On the Continent you may find that the matches are arranged in 'pools'. Draws are decided by each goalkeeper having to face a penalty flick from each member of the opposition—the best aggregate winning.

Another interesting development is spread over two days. Let us suppose that there are 16 teams.

1st Day. Four 'Pools' are arranged by teams 'drawing' for positions, and matches are only played within the 'Pool'.

2nd Day. The winners of the *previous day's 'pools'* become the new Pool 1, the runners up become Pool 2. Third place become Pool 3. Fourth place become Pool 4. Once again matches are played within the Pools. At the end of the Tournament, teams will be positioned 1–16.

The winner will be in top position in Pool 1 etc.

5th place will go to the team in top position in Pool 2 etc.

9th place will go to the team in top position in Pool 3 etc.

13th place will go to the team in top position in Pool 4 etc.

11 Equipment

THE STICK

Nowadays, the Indian-head stick has taken the place of the English-head style because it lends itself to the possibilities of reverse stick play. Being so much smaller in the head, it is much more manoeuvrable. The considerations in buying a stick are:

(1) Length.
(2) Weight.
(3) The degree of 'whip' in the handle.
(4) The size round the handle, which is an individual preference.

Schoolgirls are often in need of advice and, in my opinion, the correct length is the most important consideration. It is as essential for a beginner to feel comfortable with her stick as it is for the international. Too many times, girls are to be seen struggling with a stick far too long, or in the other extreme more senior girls, long since grown out of their original stick, inhibited and crouched over the ball never able to work up top speed.

I can well remember when I was at school often turning a somersault on the field whilst I was running—nobody seemed to attach much importance to my ignominious antics until I went to college. Fortunately, an observant coach came to my rescue—it seemed that my stick was too small, and that being faithful in keeping my hands apart for dribbling over the 'growing' years, my right hand was so far down the stick and my head so low that I was half way into a somersault whenever I ran.

There are more differences of opinion on the subject of weight. I prefer there to be a feeling of weight in the head (the degree depending on the age and build of the user), as this helps to develop the powerful drive. Do not overdo the weight, otherwise the wrists will not be able to cope with the quick manoeuvring of skilful stickwork. Although the degree of 'give' in the shaft is a personal preference, I always advise would-be purchasers to look for the whip in the handle, believing that it helps the drive; also to consider the size of the grip in relation to the size of the hand. Some players prefer the handle to be oval, others for it to be round; again it is a matter of individual preference, and with every stick being different, it is wise that each player should make her own choice. If buying in bulk, the general needs of the school or college should be assessed —bearing in mind the good points of a stick.

The ideal situation in school is to have sufficient light and short sticks with which to start the beginners and for the younger or shorter players to use; then, once having an idea of the final physique, encouraging the players to buy a stick of their own. Results will be more productive if this discussion of sticks can be timed to coincide with Christmas or birthday! However, it is necessary to have a stock of 35"–36" length and 19–20 oz. sticks for the larger players. Do label the various sticks for recognition and encourage the girls to realise the importance of the right stick.

For long life, notice the grain in the wood—if it is close together there is less likelihood of splintering and breaking away. Should this happen, it is essential and according to the rules that the stick should be bound with tape. General maintenance of sticks should include:

(1) Cleaning and oiling in the case of mulberry sticks.

(2) The waxing of ash-headed sticks.

(3) Replacing perished rubber grips.

N.B. Do not leave or store sticks in places of extreme temperature.

BALLS

These are an expensive item. The plastic variety seem to be the best buy for school use, even though they have not such a long life as the composition ball. Easy maintenance is their chief advantage. It only requires water and mild detergent to clean them and on wet days they often clean themselves. On mud they seem to run better, but there is a tendency for them to rise into the air. They sell for approx. 18/- each. For matches, leather balls are necessary and it is to be noted that the A.E.W.H.A. rule concerning balls clearly states that the cover should be of white leather. There are two varieties:

(a) The stitched ball.

(b) The seamless ball.

The seamless ball is the most popular, probably as it is the least expensive and the fact that the problem of the join coming apart is much less than with the stitched ball. The seamless ball sells for approx. 25/- and is easily obtainable. Plastic balls may be used in matches provided that it is agreed by both captains.

Maintenance of leather balls is a little more arduous for they should be painted with a quick-drying enamel paint regularly. If you have special match balls, do exchange them during matches so that they do not become too worn before receiving the next coat of paint. However, beware, some leather balls do become heavily weighted with excess paint.

The composition balls are the cheapest, selling for approximately 5/- each, but should only be used for practice purposes, and not used in a game. They are very brittle and require very regular cleaning and painting.

In frosty or snowy weather, a red leather cricket ball is a useful thing to have in school, but in these conditions avoid using the plastic cricket ball, otherwise you may have trouble with rising balls, as they are difficult to control.

For hockey in the gym, a pudding ball (a rubber texture) will prevent damage to property and have sufficient weight to give the feel of the game. These are obtainable from most large firms at approximately 10/- each.

N.B. Remember—a white ball is much easier to stop than a dirty grey one, simply because it is easier to see!

FOOTWEAR

It is interesting to see the progression from the rubber-studded or barred type of hockey boot to the more sophisticated shoe with moulded studs, for which we have to thank the development of cross-country running. They are particularly lightweight shoes with deep studs that are ideal for soft grounds and the English climate. The only disadvantage is their expense. However, for the hockey coach out in all weathers, they are a great boon, particularly to chilblain sufferers, for your feet are as dry at the end of the lesson as they were at the beginning. To be practical, the old-style boots will stay in vogue for schools for many years, mainly because they are inexpensive, but do not be surprised if the older girls take to the shoes, money is often no object to the enthusiast.

Footwear for 'all-weather surface' should be different—either the tennis shoe with a flat sole or the shallow rubber-barred variety —this will ensure that neither the pitch will be cut up, nor your knees, when the studs cause you to stumble.

CLOTHES

A well-turned-out player will certainly give a good impression and might even catch the selector's eye. This pride in appearance should be cultivated both on and off the field, whether practising or representing a team. We all know the results of a small locker stuffed with shorts, blouse, track suit, hockey boots, socks, etc., but this need not be, and what a joy it is to hear of, or see, a smartly dressed team take the field and have you noticed how much better they seem to play hockey?

That sporting clothes should be comfortable goes without saying, and now there are a variety of smart designs worth considering; of particular note are the pleated skirt and the wrap-over kilt. A.E.W.H.A. does stipulate clearly in the rules, skirts, tunics or divided skirts, and for the goalkeepers in addition the option of trousers. The skirt length should be noted; between 1 inch and 7 inches off the ground when the player kneels. The skirt style is handy in that a track suit can be worn for warm-up and then removed without undue embarrassment. At both school and club tournaments, players are sometimes to be seen breaking the Association's rules by wearing shorty shorts.

Knee-length socks are essential and a timely reminder of the value of garters does save bare legs and baggy socks around the ankles. Wool, reinforced toes and heels with nylon seem to be the most practical for they keep their absorbent quality, which is missing in all-nylon socks.

Blouses are many and various, the only point to bear in mind is that if the team wears sweaters, they should be the same colour as the blouses.

GOALKEEPING EQUIPMENT

Comfort is of prime importance. A goalkeeper has to wear more equipment than any other player but this must in no way impede her performance.

A track suit or slacks and a sweater are usually worn, a skirt is a nuisance flapping around one's knees and it is necessary to protect the backs of the legs from being chafed by the leg-guard straps. Several light, windproof layers of clothing are better than something very thick which will tend to restrict movement. Remember that a frozen goalkeeper is quite useless to her team.

Kickers

On her feet a goalkeeper wears 'kickers'; these come in various forms but there are two basic types: (a) hard shell-like leather boot covers, (b) canvas padded covers.

Type (a) may be worn over lightish shoes or boots; an old pair of lace-up walking shoes are quite suitable if studs are added to the heels as the kickers have barred or studded soles. These kickers are rather heavy and cumbersome. They protect the feet well and produce a hard kick but are rather inflexible, making directional accuracy a little difficult as the ball tends to come off at a tangent to the intended direction unless one is very careful. Some versions, with a prominent welt, act like a shovel and raise the ball dangerously.

Type (b) are worn over a fully studded football boot with a solid toe cap; they are lighter and can be strapped comfortably to the foot. They are more accurate but produce a slightly less powerful kick unless stiffened with some additional padding.

Leg-Guards (Pads)

These should be light and comfortable, preferably of a type which presents a flat front surface to the ball, i.e. those on which the straps go under the outside rolls.

It is important to have pads of the correct length to allow the knee to bend at the knee roll. Flex the lower part of the pad until it sits down snugly over the foot—this will help to bring the knee roll in the right place from the start.

Stick

A goalkeeper needs a fairly short stick, with the weight (20 ozs. maximum) well down in the head—this helps when making one-handed emergency stops at full stretch.

Gloves

If possible, wear a left-handed glove with a padded palm for stopping high shots and an ordinary leather glove on the right hand. The stick is held in the right hand for the majority of the game, the left only being added for the occasional hit or flick.

Left-handed padded gloves *are* made specially for goalkeeping, although I must admit I have only seen them for sale in the U.S.A. The alternative is to try and buy one left-handed Fives glove.

Needless to say, all this equipment will be kept spotlessly clean. A sparkling white set of pads and sweater have a magnetic effect on forwards, tempting them to shoot *at* you rather than for the corners of the goal which are hard to locate in a split second.

12 Ground Maintenance

It is very regrettable to see the general standard of pitches deteriorating. The decline is partly our fault in that most of us do not know much about the upkeep of a good playing surface, and it is left to other people who probably have not the time, interest or finance to care for it properly. So for reference purposes, I have included this section.

Maintenance:

(1) *Regular close mowing and rolling.* A gang mower every now and again is most unsatisfactory and a situation many clubs and schools are having to accept. Regular rolling is more important than heavy rolling, although the latter is very helpful in dry spells to flatten the mounds. (Do not ask for the heavy roller, when the tractor will leave its tracks all over the field.) The ideal is to run a motor mower over the field once a week, even when the grass stops growing, as the rollers will help to flatten divots. Both the following and mowing should be done in both directions during the course of maintenance.

(2) *Regular Spiking* is ideal for it because it

(a) gives longer periods of play as it helps to drain the top surface.

(b) stimulates the growth of the grass, aerates the turf and improves the general texture.

(3) Treat the goal-mouths and other worn areas with sand on wet days. It will assist drainage and ensure the goalkeepers of a reasonable footing. (Sawdust is cloggy and not to be recommended.)

(4) To improve a surface:

(A) Lay 'Top Dressing' annually, and this is best done in the summer months: 5 tons to an acre is considered adequate. It is a well-worth-while procedure even if it does have to come out of private funds. It will help to prevent a glutinous mud in the depths of winter.

(B) In the summer holidays treat the fields with 'Autumn Dressing'; this incorporates a fertilizer which will improve the quality of the grass.

(C) Move the pitches each season. If space is no problem, the ideal is to be able to turn them sideways. For the less fortunate, a few yards both ways will ensure a fresh goal mouth.

(D) Treat the worn areas either by re-turfing or re-seeding ready for the following season.

(5) It is advisable to seek specialist advice when weeds, worms or fungus spoil the playing surface.

INDEX